66 What you say to your children will greatly influence the way they view themselves and their world. In *Pinocchio Parenting*, Chuck Borsellino may help you discover that you are telling your children more lies than you realize, and some of them may be whoppers!"

GARY D. CHAPMAN, PHD—Best-Selling Author of
The Five Love Languages

66 *Pinocchio Parenting* by Chuck Borsellino is more than just another how-to-parent-your-children-the-right-way sort of book. It's wisdom, experience, and common sense all rolled into one, and you'll be doing yourself a service if you not only read the book but put the advice to work when it comes to raising your children."

NICHOLAS SPARKS—Best-Selling Author of *A Walk to Remember*
and *The Notebook*, Father of Five

66 While reading *Pinocchio Parenting*, I felt my own nose growing as I tried to convince myself I'd never told my kids a fib . . . *ha!* Chuck's witty approach and wise advice make this book a joy to read. Filled with memorable examples, practical ideas, and wisdom honed from years of counseling and fathering, Chuck offers readers the vital tools they need to help their kids face the Real World by consistently speaking the truth in love. A timely, much-needed guide for every parent."

LIZ CURTIS HIGGS—Best-Selling Author of *Bad Girls of the Bible*

66 Chuck Borsellino has written the book that every pastor and parent needs. When I read the manuscript, the ideas immediately became a part of my thinking, speaking, and writing. This book is informative, interesting, exciting, and . . . necessary. I have thousands of books in my library, but none of them deal with these issues. Good job, Dr. Borsellino! This one is a home run!"

PASTOR TED HAGGARD—President of the National
Association of Evangelicals (NAE)

" Chuck is one of the most brilliant men I know, with an uncanny ability to make abstract concepts very practical and concrete. This is a great book for us dads and you moms. It rips through the false perceptions that destroy lives, and it preserves the truth that can transform our kids!"

STEPHEN ARTERBURN—Best-Selling Author of the
Every Man's Series and *Healing Is a Choice*

" Once I picked up *Pinocchio Parenting*, I couldn't put it down. Combining his unique wit with his keen insight as a practicing psychologist, Chuck Borsellino exposes the lies we've all told our children. Instead of piling on heaps of guilt, *Pinocchio Parenting* offers practical helps for communicating life's most important truths to our kids. This book is a must-read for every mom and dad."

DR. ROBERT JEFFRESS—Pastor and Best-Selling Author of *Hell? Yes!*

" This book will help parents negotiate that squishy ground between platitude and reality and help them dive into some uncomfortable tensions. In a time when kids need honest conversations like never before, this book is a helpful tool to parents on how to think through some of those conversations. Thanks, Chuck, for giving us some good things to think about!"

DR. HENRY CLOUD—Best-Selling Author of *Boundaries*

" I'm guilty of *Pinocchio Parenting*. The sad truth is, I actually believed some of these lies myself. Thank you, Chuck Borsellino, for both convicting and convincing me. This book is a blessing for any parent willing to be honest with themselves and their children—I'm not lying!"

LISA WHELCHEL—Best-Selling Author of *The Busy Mom's Guide to Prayer, Creative Correction, The Facts of Life and Other Lessons My Father Taught Me*, and *Taking Care of the "Me" in Mommy*

Chuck Borsellino
PhD, PsyD

Pinocchio
Parenting

21 OUTRAGEOUS LIES WE
TELL OUR KIDS

HOST
OF TV'S
AT HOME—
LIVE!

HOWARD BOOKS
A DIVISION OF SIMON & SCHUSTER
NEW YORK LONDON TORONTO SIDNEY

Our purpose at Howard Books is to:

- *Increase faith* in the hearts of growing Christians
- *Inspire holiness* in the lives of believers
- *Instill hope* in the hearts of struggling people everywhere

Because He's coming again!

HOWARD
BOOKS

Published by Howard Books, a division of Simon & Schuster
1230 Avenue of the Americas, New York, NY 10020

Pinocchio Parenting © 2006 by Chuck Borsellino
In association with the literary agency of
Alive Communications, Inc. 7680 Goddard Street, Suite 200,
Colorado Springs, CO 80920

Library of Congress Cataloging-in-Publication Data

Borsellino, Chuck.
    Pinocchio parenting : 21 outrageous lies we tell our kids / Chuck Borsellino.
        p. cm.
    Includes bibliographical references.
    ISBN 13: 978-1-58229-572-5
    ISBN 10: 1-58229-572-7
    1. Parenting—Psychological aspects. 2. Child rearing—Psychological aspects. 3.
Parent and child. 4. Truthfulness and falsehood. 5. Communication in the family. I.
Title.

HQ755.8.B665 2006
649'.7—dc22

                                                                    20006043456

10 9 8 7 6 5 4 3 2 1

HOWARD is a registered trademark of Simon & Schuster, Inc.

Manufactured in the United States of America

For information regarding special discounts for bulk purchases, please contact Simon & Schuster
Special Sales at 1-800-456-6798 or business@simonandschuster.com

Edited by Michele Buckingham
Interior design by Stephanie D. Walker
Cover design by David Carlson

I dedicate this book . . .
To the tireless moms and dads living in the trenches of parenthood. Be applauded: despite what they say, you're doing the right thing.

To the three kids in my life who turned textbook theories into tried and tested wisdom. Be commended: you turned a man into a dad.

To my wife of twenty-eight years. You never gave up on me. You never let go of me. You never stopped loving me. Be prepared: someday you will be sainted.

To my Father who promised me abundant life here on earth and eternal life when I leave. Be praised: this trip has been incredible . . . I can only imagine the future.

To you, the one who cracked the cover of this book hoping to find help for your home and hope for your heart. Be encouraged: the truth will set you free.

Contents

Introduction

The Truth about the Lies We Tell

SMART PEOPLE BELIEVE HALF OF WHAT THEY HEAR.
REALLY SMART PEOPLE KNOW WHICH HALF TO BELIEVE.

The truth is, everybody lies. Deny it, and you're probably lying. Small lies are called "fibs." Big ones are called "whoppers." Necessary ones are called "white." For politicians, lying has been perfected to an art form. For parents, it's more of a necessity:

"Your mommy and I were just wrestling . . ."

"Your fish went to live with their friends in the ocean."

"If you keep making that face, it's going to stay that way."

"Tell me the truth, and I promise I won't get mad. YOU BROKE WHAT?"

We live in a culture where lying is commonplace—just as fish live in a culture where wet is the norm. According to the book *The Day America Told the Truth*, 91 percent of Americans surveyed admitted to lying routinely: 86 percent lie to parents, 75 percent lie to friends, 73 percent lie to siblings, and 69 percent lie to spouses ("Oh this old thing—I've had it for ages.")

On average we lie about twice a day.[1] That's more often than most people brush their teeth.

We've become a nation of what I call "Pinocchio people." When our backs are against the wall, the lies seem to slide off the tips of our tongues—and our noses grow a little bit longer:

- Money lies: "The check is in the mail."

- Math lies: "I just turned thirty-nine."

- Medical lies: "The doctor will call you right back."

- Work lies: "I can't come in to work today. I think I have diphtheria."

- Social lies: "It's delicious, but I just can't eat another bite."

- Advertising lies: "Melt away ten pounds in just ten minutes!"

- Dating lies: "I had a great time. I'll call you tomorrow."

- And necessary lies: "Fat? No, honey, you look great in that dress."

To lie has become as American as apple pie. We lie to protect ourselves; we lie to promote ourselves. We lie when it's convenient; we lie when we're caught.

According to the Bureau of Labor Statistics, each year more than 10 million taxpayers lie to the IRS, 6.6 million job applicants lie on their resumes, 300,000 doctors lie to health insurance providers, and 490,000 lawyers in America admit that they distort the truth in order to aid their clients and win their cases.[2] (By the way, how do you know when a lawyer is lying? Some people say it's when their lips are moving.)

One Sunday a minister concluded his sermon by saying,

"Next Sunday I'm going to be speaking on the ninth Commandment: "Thou shalt not lie." In preparation for the lesson, I want each member of the congregation to read the seventeenth chapter of Mark."

The following Sunday the minister said, "Last Sunday I asked each of you to read the seventeenth chapter of Mark in preparation for this morning's service. If you read the seventeenth chapter of Mark, please raise your hand." Nearly every hand in the congregation went up.

Then the minister said, "Those of you who didn't raise your hands can go home. Those who did raise your hands are the ones I want to talk to this morning. There is no seventeenth chapter of Mark."

Dr. Bella DePaulo, a psychologist at the University of Virginia, concluded that some relationships are virtual magnets for deception. The worst? Parent-teenager relationships. "College students lie to their mothers in one out of two conversations," DePaulo discovered.[3] As a father of a college student, I find that revelation rather eye opening.

The proverbial ball, however, isn't only in the teenage court. Unfortunately, most of us parents have taken the "license to lie" to our children to new levels. Not intentionally, mind you; but unintentional distortions have the same consequences— damage that's done to us, as well as to our kids. Damage that ruins our credibility and warps their reality.

We've become "Pinocchio parents"—and our parental noses just keep getting longer:

- "It's not your fault."
- "God helps those who help themselves."
- "Honey, you can be anything you want to be."

- "When I was your age, I walked to school in the snow . . . without shoes . . . uphill both ways!"

Really?

Living by the Lie

According to psychologist Dr. Chris Thurman, most of us are "living by the lie." In his book *The Lies We Believe*, Thurman makes the case that we become what we believe. He concludes that while circumstances affect our lives, it is our beliefs about those circumstances that give birth to our behaviors.[4] Steve Chandler, author of *Seventeen Lies That Are Holding You Back and the Truth That Will Set You Free*, agrees. Our beliefs, not our feelings, are what determine our behaviors, he says. In the same manner our feelings are no more the cause of our problems than the red spots on our faces are the cause of our measles. Feelings are not the source of problems; they are the result.[5]

So if beliefs determine behavior, where do our beliefs come from? Well, in most cases they are suggested by good ol' Mom and Dad. That's right—well-intentioned parents that innocently tell tales to their kids. Parents like you and me.

Of course, our purposes are noble. In most cases they are designed to:

- Make sense of our circumstances ("It's not whether you win or lose—it's how you play the game.")

- Bring assurance to our anxieties ("It's not your fault.")

- Inspire our kids to live beyond their limits ("You can be anything you want to be.")

Unfortunately, the little lies, fibs, and clichés we tell our kids today become the beliefs that shape their behaviors tomorrow. Want a few examples? Although the names are changed, each of the following stories is true.

Darrin is a typical seventeen-year-old, five-foot-eleven teenager who would rather play basketball than crack open his chemistry book. He barely passed the eleventh grade. It doesn't matter though; Darrin is counting on playing basketball in the NBA . . . for the Detroit Pistons. Well-intentioned parents wanting to motivate Darrin told him to "dream big," because one day all his dreams would come true.

His belief: "If I dream it, I can do it."

Melody is a seven-year-old girl who is confused about God. Since she can remember, her parents told her there is a God in heaven. She's not so sure anymore. Since she can remember, her parents also told her there's a Santa Claus at the North Pole. But recently, when Melody shared with her friends at school what she wanted from Santa for Christmas, they laughed at her.

Her belief: "I can't tell when Mommy and Daddy are telling the truth—or when they're telling a tale."

Jessica is a bright but insecure eighteen-year-old high-school senior who has worked hard to maintain her A average. Unfortunately, socializing has never come easily for her. Her parents were so pleased with her success in school that they promised her they would give her whatever she wanted for graduation. When she said, "I want breast implants," they said, "OK."

Her belief, reinforced by her parents' quick acceptance of her request: "My social status will increase with my chest size."

Twenty-two-year-old Eric sits on the sidelines of life waiting for his big break. He was voted Most Likely to Succeed in high school but completed only two years of college before dropping out. He has failed to keep a permanent job ever since. Today he spends most of his time sleeping and waiting for success to come knocking—when he wins the lottery. After all, his parents always told him he had "unlimited potential" and that someday he was going to "make it big."

> His belief: "It's easier to live on my potential
> than to pursue a goal and fail."

Conner has his marital back against the wall. He's been married for four years. While he loves Lisa very much, he never buys her a birthday gift or anniversary card. He always has an excuse—just like his father did. Conner's mother was an enabler who used to pardon his dad's practice with the cliché, "That's OK. It's the thought that counts." Conner's wife isn't so . . . understanding.

> His belief:
> "Like father, like son—that's the way I was raised.
> My mother was OK with it.
> Lisa just needs to be more understanding."

I've been a therapist now for over twenty-five years, first as a marriage and family therapist, then as a clinical psychologist. Over the years I've seen each of these situations in therapy. My conclusion: behind each unhealthy behavior is an unhealthy belief, whether conscious or not.

Beliefs determine behavior. That means that the key to changing behavior is to change beliefs—to exchange unhealthy or unrealistic beliefs for healthy, realistic ones. It's really quite simple: change unhealthy beliefs, and you'll change unhealthy behavior.

In each of the previous examples, these kids were good kids—but also misdirected kids. They had good parents, but misguided parents. As a psychologist, I've sat with many troubled teens and puzzled parents, and I can tell you this: Most parents aren't mean—but many are misled. Most kids aren't mindless—but many are misinformed.

Generally speaking, parents are well intentioned. We do our best to create a family environment that will protect our kids when they're young and prepare them for when they're older. We do what we can to provide them with a healthy diet of motivation, encouragement, and support. But sometimes we end up feeding them "ideas" that are helpful in the short run but harmful for their future—motivational snacks that soothe the spirit but spoil the main meal; snacks that not only contaminate their beliefs but discredit the cook.

True Lies

In most cases we're simply repeating the clichés we heard from our own parents when we were growing up. *If it was good for me, it will be good for them,* we figure. We don't stop and think, *But is it true?* We assume the clichés, half-truths, and tales we share will motivate the motionless and bring clarity to the confused. Just what our kids need, right?

The trouble with our tales is that many of them contain a little bit of fact and a little bit of fiction. Subconsciously we hope the fact outweighs the fiction, because believing the tale would make everything seem OK. But it's not OK. Believing a lie doesn't make it the truth. That's the first problem.

The second problem is this: because a lie often contains an

element of truth, spotting the lie is difficult. If it's sometimes true, is it always true? Where does the truth end and the lie begin? If only the lie jumped out from the truth and made itself known! Unfortunately, it doesn't. It's like distinguishing salt and sugar. Distinguishing salt from pepper is easy; distinguishing salt from sugar is much more difficult. But just because two things are hard to distinguish doesn't mean they go together.

Finally, we're creatures of habit. We repeat what we hear but fail to examine what we believe. As a result, we perpetuate the problem by passing on the tales we've heard without giving them much thought. After all, the ones who told us these tales were honest, sincere, loving people, right? They were *our parents*. Surely they wouldn't lie to us . . . would they?

No, not intentionally. But honest, sincere, loving parents are not always right—even if they are honest, sincere, and loving. Honest.

Perhaps you have this book in your hand right now because you're curious. You're thinking to yourself, *Am I a Pinocchio parent? What lies, tales, and clichés do I tell my kids? How do these lies hurt them? How do they hurt me?*

In the pages that follow, we're going to examine twenty-one of the most common lies, half-truths, tales, and clichés that roll off the tips of our parental tongues. We'll sort out fact from fiction, intention from outcome. You see, passing on lies to our kids because "they sound good" or because "that's what my mom and dad told me" will only make our noses grow longer. One day our children just may notice our Pinocchio noses and yell, "Liar, liar, parents on fire!"

This is a disorder that can be extinguished.

THE LIE

You Can Be Anything You Want to Be

"OK, THEN, I WANT TO BE WONDER WOMAN."
Debbie Borsellino, age seven

Business was brisk. The sign in the window said it all: "We'll make you whoever you want to be." Outside, the line was long; inside, the options were limitless: supermodel, Supreme Court justice, or Sleeping Beauty. The process was painless: make your selection, pay your fee, and live the dream. Excitement filled the air as lives were converted from plumber to president, from window washer to Wonder Woman. Unfortunately, the transformations were temporary. The sign over the door read Rick's Halloween Costumes. The fine print on the receipt read "All costumes must be returned by Tuesday."

When I was growing up, Halloween was an opportunity to suspend the realities of life and become anybody I wanted to be . . . at least for one night. It was about more than trading costumes for candy; it was about trading fact for fantasy. Even if it only lasted a day, it was unforgettable!

You don't have to be a Harvard-trained psychologist to realize that costume choices say a lot about a person's dreams and desires. When I was eight, I was a black bear. At nine I was one of the Beatles. By eleven I was a pirate, fully equipped with eye patch, hand hook, sword, pistol, and Mace (just in case). That was the year my parents took note of my gradual decline from black bear to Blackbeard. That was also the year they began to pray for me—I'm talking on your knees, hands clasped, eyes closed, "We need a miracle" kind of prayer. Fasting was soon to follow!

Not long after that, Halloween changed. Halloween was "for kids," and dressing up was for the innocent or the immature. Nevertheless, one Halloween message survived long after the costumes were tucked away in the hallway closet: "You can be anything you want to be." All I had to do was dream it and then become it.

OK, then, I want to be Brad Pitt!
That's when I noticed that noses began to grow.

Jennifer's parents didn't mean for it to happen, but their noses were growing too. Jennifer was barely out of diapers when she was told to dream beyond her limits. Not just to do something significant with her life . . . but something supernatural. Her well-intentioned parents told her that she was destined for distinction. They said she could be anything she wanted to be, and Jennifer believed them. That's when five-year-old Jennifer surveyed the landscape of possibilities and made a decision. While watching a football game one Sunday afternoon with her dad, Jennifer decided to become a Dallas Cowboys cheerleader. Why not?

Throughout her early years Jennifer's parents enrolled her in jazz and gymnastics classes, followed by two years of dance classes. She was told that she had "potential," but on the floor there was little evidence. In the seventh grade Jennifer began sixteen months of cheerleading lessons at Champion Cheer. Then it was time to fulfill her destiny and begin her march to Cowboys Stadium by first becoming a high-school cheerleader.

Easier said than done.

Jennifer was dismissed during the first round of competition in the ninth grade. Her lessons continued. She made it to the second round in the tenth grade, when the judges said, "Try again next year." Disappointed but still dreaming, she made her way back to cheer school.

Finally, it was time to shine or get off the stage. Jennifer tried out one more time in the eleventh grade. Unfortunately, the results were the same. Apparently, her five-foot-eight, 134-pound frame was her enemy—not her ally. Jennifer's ankles couldn't handle the impact of landing her round-off back handsprings. Braces increased her support, ice decreased her swelling . . . but nothing provided a solution. Her heart was broken, her dream was shattered, and her belief in the "dream it and do it" theory was crushed.

Getting Wise to the Lies

During his nationally televised presidential nomination speech in 1996, Bob Dole stated that 74 percent of all Americans believe that with hard work, "you can be anything you want to be."[1] He said it; we believe it. Unfortunately, that doesn't change the facts. Let's check the fine print:

- It may be conceivably true . . . after all, 74 percent believe it.

- It may be partially true . . . dreams do begin with desire.

- It may be relatively true . . . it's easier to achieve your dreams in America than anywhere else.

- But it's not absolutely true . . . even though that's the way we tell it.

It's a belief that's fashionable, but not factual. Whether we like it or not, birds don't swim, fish don't fly, and basketball superstars don't make baseball players, even when their name is Michael Jordan.

Michael Jordan had a lifelong desire to play major-league baseball. With his basketball achievements behind him, his baseball aspirations before him, and his athletic abilities within him, he stepped into the batter's box—and found out during the next two agonizing years that he couldn't hit a curve ball. The Chicago Bulls were delighted; Michael gave up baseball, returned to basketball, and led them to another NBA World Championship.

Someone like Marcus Buckingham could have saved him a lot of trouble. In his best-selling book *Now, Discover Your Strengths*, Buckingham challenges the notion that anyone can learn to be anything he or she wants to be. He asserts that one of the most significant variables that propels a person from average to awesome is neither skill nor knowledge, but talent. Skill and knowledge can be developed, but talent is unique, enduring, and resistant to change. According to Buckingham, teaching kids that they can be anything they want to be minimizes their individuality and suggests that each child is merely a blank sheet of paper. One page just like the other 499 in the pack of 500. A piece of copy paper for the printer rather than an individually cut diamond for the jeweler.[2]

Arthur Miller puts it this way in his book *Why You Can't Be Anything You Want to Be*: education may help develop your mind, the church may help define your calling, motivation may help drive your dream, and the workplace may help direct your skills; but ultimately, success is based more on your unique abilities than your personal desires.[3] After all, if anybody can be anything, then the only difference between a nurse and a neurosurgeon is personal choice (and their paychecks).

Recently I had the opportunity to sit with a highly skilled cardiologist. Not in an operating room, but in a television studio. Not between surgeries, but between stories. Max Lucado is an author who can touch the human heart with a word better than a heart surgeon can with a scalpel. He's a publishing phenomenon with more than forty million books in print. He can make a story come to life better than Broadway. Maybe that's why *Reader's Digest* declared him "Best Preacher in America."[4] For fifteen years I knew Max from a distance, as I devoured most of his manuscripts. During the past five years I've gotten to know the person behind the pen, as I've interviewed him several times in the studio. The first fifteen years were like hamburger; the last five have been like filet.

The focus of our recent interview was his book called *Cure for the Common Life: Living in Your Sweet Spot*. In it Max comes to the same conclusion others have: you simply cannot be anything you want to be. That you *can* is a lie that trickles into many a preacher's teaching. But as Max points out, God created each person to be "you-nique." To one he gave an eye for organization, to another an ear for music, and to another a mind that understands quantum physics. Would Beethoven have made a better chemist than composer? Could you imagine Picasso as an accomplished accountant? The numbers just wouldn't have lined up—literally! Lucado asks, "Can an acorn become a rose, a whale fly like a bird, or lead become gold?"[5]

The Bible asks a similar question: "Can the Ethiopian change his skin or the leopard his spots?" (Jeremiah 13:23).

TRUTH OR CONSEQUENCES

Believing a lie is the first step toward living it. Remember, our behaviors are driven by our beliefs. The fact is, following this particular lie will lead our kids down the path to personal disappointment, causing them to question both the message and the messenger. We want to motivate our kids to dream big and reach for their goals, but this tale goes over the line.

THE TRUTH

You may not be able to be anything
you want to be in life, but you can do
the most you can with what you have
and do it in a way nobody
has ever seen before.

My son isn't a superstar; my daughter isn't a supermodel . . . and I'm no closer to being Brad Pitt. For years my sister wanted to be Wonder Woman, but the tights never fit. Clearly, we *can't* be anything we want to be in life, despite what many well-intentioned people say. It's time to call this concept a fable, not a fact.

I'm not suggesting that we stop encouraging our children to have big dreams, but let's teach them to dream with their eyes open and their feet on the ground, rather than with their eyes closed and their fingers crossed behind their backs. Let's teach them how to develop the gifts and talents God has given them instead of trying to become something or someone they were never intended to be.

My dad was a welder. He worked at Proctor & Gamble as a welder for most of his life. He was probably the smartest guy I have ever known . . . and he didn't make it past the ninth grade. Times were different when my dad grew up. Destinies were determined by World War I, the Depression, and World War II. Putting food on the table and clothes on our backs was more important to him than academic achievement or self-actualization.

My parent's grew up to obligations; I grew up to options.

I don't remember my parents telling me, "You can be anything you want to be," but I knew kids whose parents did. Instead, my parents told me that God had a dream for my life and that if I lived for him, he'd fulfill that dream. So while my high-school grades were less than stellar, I discovered they were good enough to pry open the door to college. A bachelor's degree led to a master's degree, a master's degree led to a doctoral degree, and that doctoral degree led to another. (The truth is, I'm not that bright; but I did figure out that going to school was a great way to avoid work!)

Today I find myself living the dream I would have never dared to ask for. On many mornings I pinch myself on the way to the television studio. I didn't get here by living my life believing I could be anything I wanted to be. Instead, I got here by living my life for the One who said, "I know the plans I have for you . . . plans to prosper you and not to harm you, plans to give you hope and a future" (Jeremiah 29:11 NIV).

> I offered God kindling;
> he made a castle and gave me the keys.

As parents we all want the best for our kids. We want them to experience success in life . . . to "live the dream." To this end let me offer a few suggestions:

1. *Resist the Pinocchio pretence of telling your kids they can be anything they want to be.* They can't. But don't stop with what you *don't* tell them; be intentional and proactive in what you *do* tell them: God has a plan and purpose for their lives. Help them discover and pursue it with everything they've got.

2. *Encourage your kids to do their very best at whatever they try to do.* Remind them that they don't have to be *the* best, just *their* best. Give them plenty of praise and reward effort, not just outcome.

3. *Encourage your kids to set their goals high.* All kids have certain limitations, but that doesn't mean they can't set goals that reach beyond them. Give God a chance to show up and take your kids from "their best" to "his best."

4. *Motivate your children to work hard to accomplish their goals.* Talent is a significant factor in goal achievement, but don't discount effort and endurance. If your kids can't outsmart or outskill those around them, they can always outwork them.

5. *Encourage your children to try lots of different things:* play in the band, join the soccer team, take an art class, check out the chess club. That's how they'll discover their own unique set of God-given gifts. God has packed our kids' bags with specific talents, gifts, interests, and desires—all for a purpose. Part of our role as parents is to help them identify and pursue that purpose, not teach them to duplicate someone else's.

When you tell your kids the truth about who they are and what they can become, you're not limiting them. On the contrary, you're teaching them that with God's help, their destination can be better than they ever dreamed—it's just not likely to include becoming a goldfish. Sorry, Josh!

Oh yeah, remember Jennifer and her dream to cheer? Her parents finally concluded that goals, gifts, and God are what make dreams happen. Jennifer had the goal but not the gift. Maybe God was pointing her in another direction. They encouraged Jennifer to ask God for a new dream—one that utilized the gifts he had given her.

As a result, as one door closed, another door opened. Just like cheering, this door led to the football field—but as a member of the marching band. Jennifer had been playing the clarinet since she was fourteen. Her talent was unmistakable; her gift was unquestionable. Both made her position with the band undeniable.

It was her God-given gift, not just her goal,
that took Jennifer from the sidelines to centerfield.

The musical talent that Jennifer applied to the marching band marched her to college and beyond. She received a music scholarship to attend Texas Christian University. She is currently a member of the Saint Louis Philharmonic.

THE LIE

Looks Don't Matter— It's What's on the Inside That Counts

GOD LOOKS ON THE INSIDE FOR THE THINGS THAT MATTER MOST.
UNFORTUNATELY, HE MAY BE THE ONLY ONE WHO DOES.

Want to find a financial planner? Check the Yellow Pages. Want to find a car? Check the classifieds. What to find a soul mate? Better contact eHarmony.com. Want to find a financial planner—with a new car—for a romantic encounter? Look in the personal ads:

> Her name is Kelli. She describes herself as a "beautiful, buxom blonde." She's a thirty-seven-year-old SWF who recently moved from Chattanooga to Dallas and is looking for a "tall and trim, affluent businessman who's into traveling, eating out, and fantasy fulfillment." Meet the criteria . . . and you could be fulfilling your fantasy with Kelli this Friday. Just be sure to send a photo.

> Hmmm.

His name is Chris. He describes himself as an "incurable romantic who's financially successful and emotionally sensitive." He's a forty-one-year-old DWM who's looking for a "special" woman. According to Chris, *special* means "twenty to thirty years old, smart, slim, and sexy." If you like sailing, skiing, and other water sports, send a photo . . . "in your water-wear."

Double hmmm.

What's Love Got to Do with It?

Personal ads are an important source of insight and information about modern dating and mating strategies. Despite the unlimited opportunities to "meet-a-mate" at the hunting grounds of our forefathers (the workplace and church), and despite the continued popularity of singles bars, many busy, high-tech singles have upgraded to personal ads, speed dating, and e-mating. Regardless of the meeting method, however, the research is consistent: physical appearance is still the number one criteria *du jour*. That's right . . . even though most will admit that our culture's preoccupation with the packaging is shallow—kiddie-pool, puddle-on-the-driveway shallow—looks matter!

Over the years numerous studies have been conducted on the role of physical attractiveness in the dating process, and the results are "abundant, convincing, and overwhelming": what's on the outside trumps what's on the inside, hands down.[1] We all know that superficiality is the rule for Shallow Hal and other mindless men like him—but women? Yep. Despite the fact that most women say they want to date a "kind and sensitive" man, their actions speak louder than their words. Just like men, they tend to choose a book for the cover, not the content.[2]

The Beauty Bias

In their revealing book, *Mirror, Mirror: The Importance of Looks in Everyday Life*, psychologists Elaine Hatfield and Susan Sprecher point out that while beauty may be in the eye of the beholder, most of America is biased by beauty.[3] In fact, according to research, attractive people are most likely to be perceived as:

- Friendly

- Sociable

- Competent

- Popular

- Self-confident

- More likely to succeed

- Better adjusted

- Better liked

- More socially skilled

- Mentally healthier[4]

Meanwhile, the less attractive or overweight are frequently perceived as:

- Lazy

- Simple-minded

- Lonely

- Dependent

- Insecure

- Complaisant[5]

And if you think adults are the only ones affected by the beauty bias, think again.

Trish is a mother of two. Her fourteen-year-old daughter, Jenna, is an average student with a thin build, big brown eyes, and thick dark hair. Jenna can't keep up with her countless social invitations—sleepovers, birthday parties, movies, and trips to the mall—while her fifteen-year-old sister, Shelley, sits on the social sidelines. Shelley is an A student who has braces on her teeth, glasses for her eyes, and a pituitary disorder that renders her seventy pounds overweight. Friends are few and rejections are familiar. She has a broken spirit; her mother has a broken heart. They don't say it out loud, but neither is optimistic that Shelley's future will be any different from the past.

"That's OK; it's what's on the inside that really counts," Trish tells Shelley, hoping to soothe her pain and encourage her spirits. Unfortunately, she's not being altogether truthful—and both mother and daughter know it. They can deny it. They can complain about it. But they can't change the basic fact that looks make a difference.

Unfortunately, looks not only make a difference socially, they also make a difference academically. Research has shown that at school, teachers ascribe a "halo effect" to the buffed, the bronzed, and the beautiful. They tend to treat good-looking students as if they're little angels—whether or not they really are. More specifically, teachers' expectations are higher for good-looking students . . . and students tend to live up to their expectations.[6] It's a self-fulfilling prophecy. In fact, in a study of student attitudes, researchers found that most students believed that attractive students were successful because of effort and ability. Those less attractive were deemed successful because of luck.[7]

Once you leave the classroom and graduate to the boardroom, things only get worse. First of all, attractive candidates consistently receive higher interview ratings than those deemed less attractive and are therefore more likely to be hired.[8] Attractive employees are described as more assertive and more accepted by their coworkers, while less attractive employees are described as less intelligent, less popular, less active, and less likely to succeed[9]—overall, they are seen as just plain "less."

Jennifer Portnick, on the other hand, was just plain more. This forty-one-year-old mom is a personal trainer and fitness instructor. She taught intermediate aerobics classes at World Gym for months, but when she applied to become a Jazzercise franchisee, she was denied. The reason? Body image. Jennifer weighed 240 pounds. She filed a suit against the company for discrimination. They dropped their policy. She dropped her suit.[10]

Unfortunately, the bias that began on the playground also has a profound impact on your paycheck. A recent study by the Federal Reserve Bank of St. Louis found that a worker with below-average looks earned about 9 percent less per hour than a coworker who was viewed as above average in appearance. And it's not just a pretty face that helps boost wages. A poll of half of all Fortune 500 companies found that their CEOs are almost three inches taller than the average American.[11]

Thanks, Dad!

And by the way, how long does it take for someone to form an opinion about you? *Four minutes*. That's right. It takes about four minutes for someone to form a lasting impression about you[12]—and 65 percent of that impression is based on your appearance.[13] First impressions are critical!

TRUTH OR CONSEQUENCES

Here's my point: whether the setting is the classroom or the boardroom, messages are sent by your appearance long before your words are ever heard. Unfortunately, many people will discount the quality of your competence and the caliber of your character simply because of the nature of your appearance. Looks may not matter to God, but they seem to matter to almost everyone else.

THE TRUTH

Appearance is important.
First impressions are fast and
unforgettable, so do what you can to
make them count, not cost.

For years I've preached the importance of competence and character. Competence is what you do; character is who you are. Together they form the foundation for your future. Unfortunately, they're not the only things that matter.

As a psychologist I'll be the first to tell you that "it's what's on the inside that counts." But as an author I also know that "covers sell books." The cover compels a window shopper to go further . . . or go fish. Appearance works the same way. To tell our kids that looks don't matter is simply not true. It only makes our noses grow longer. The truth is, if they don't pay a healthy, reasonable amount of attention to their outward appearance, there's no question that their potential for social, academic, and vocational success will be affected.

Don't misunderstand me. If I had to choose a book based on its cover *or* on its content, I'd choose content, hands down. Content will keep my interest and feed my mind long after the glitter of the cover wears off. But publishers know the importance of catching the eye of the buyer, and they will spend great amounts of time and resources creating a cover that will help convert a scanner into a buyer. A creative title and cover get the book off the shelf and into the hand; a critique of the content gets it to the cash register.

With people, competence and character are the qualities that count over the long haul. They are the substance that relationships are built on. They sustain and satisfy our craving for connection long after the glitter of the "cover" wears off. But here's the point: it will be your "cover" that opens the door; it will be your "content" that keeps you there. Strive for both! Appearance matters—no matter how loudly we protest . . . no matter how shallow it seems. We must not mislead our children to believe that appearance is irrelevant. It's not.

Just ask Kelli and Chris. Personally, I don't know if Kelli or Chris ever found what they were looking for, but word on the street was that Kelly wasn't exactly the "buxom bombshell" she advertised, and Chris was "financially successful"—only if you think in terms of tips from pizza deliveries. Whatever happened to truth in advertising?

Dressing for Success

Parenting in this area is a challenge. Overemphasize appearance, and your kids become superficial, focused primarily on the external. Underemphasize appearance, and your kids are discounted academically, socially, and vocationally. In order to "dress your kids for success," you need to help them find the right balance between these two opposing forces. That's no easy task—kind of like buying fashion without paying a fortune.

Many helpful and not-so-helpful professionals offer a smorgasbord of treats and treatments to assist you. Appetizers include braces for crooked teeth and implants for missing ones; dermatologists for blemished skin and tanning salons for the white-skinned. Main-meal options include an array of plastic-surgery procedures and a "solution" for every imperfection: liposuction for the "full-figured," breast augmentation for the "less-figured," and rhinoplasty for the disfigured. For dessert there are personal trainers, makeup artists, hair stylists, clothing experts, and nutritionists who can be added a la carte.

Did I miss anybody?

As the parent it's your responsibility to make balanced, healthy menu choices for your children. It's up to you to discern what's wanted, what's needed, and what's simply wished for. In addition to financial constraints, you must consider which "adjustments" or "add-ons" will be helpful and which will ultimately be harmful to a specific child's physical, emotional, mental, and spiritual well-being. When it comes to raising prepared kids, not just pretty kids, balance is the key.

Here are some suggestions for helping your children find that healthy balance between caring for what's on the inside and what's on the outside:

1. *Major on "health"; minor on "beauty."* Emphasize healthy eating and regular exercise so that your kids learn to value fitness, not vanity. Everything from weight management

to hygiene, skin care to smoking, can all be couched in terms of "What's the healthy thing to do?"

2. *Replace snack foods with healthy foods.* If it's not in the pantry, it can't find its way to their stomachs. You may not be able to control everything that finds its way to their mouths, but you can manage most of the options they find in your house.

3. *Consider the following as investments, not expenses:* orthodontists for braces, dermatologists for skin care, stylists for hair care, and even plastic surgeons for cosmetic repairs. Notice I said "repairs," not "enhancements"— the first deals with a *restoration*, the second deals with a *fixation*. Anything can be taken too far, including the pursuit of physical "perfection."

4. *Understand there will be times to sacrifice and times to save.* When investing in your children's appearance, never accept that you must live beyond your financial means in order to provide for their fashion *wants*. On the other hand, there may be times when it's appropriate to spend beyond your comfort level in order to provide for their legitimate *needs*.

5. *Spend money on staples; save money on trends, when it comes to shopping for clothes.* Your kids need to understand that if they march to the drum of the fashion industry, their closets may be full, but your wallet will be empty. That's not good stewardship. Teach them to compare cost and consequences, fit and fashion, by letting them know there is a budget for back-to-school clothes. Then ask, "Now, which choice do you think would be best, given

the money we have to spend?" Start early and repeat often!

6. *Remember that nothing speaks louder than your example.* Kids learn more with their eyes than their ears. They'll follow your footsteps faster than your words. Model the behaviors you want them to follow: Eat right. Exercise often. Dress smart. Your kids are taking notes!

Remember Trish, Jenna, and Shelley? Well, Trish took these suggestions to heart and began encouraging her daughters to eat and exercise for health reasons, not vanity reasons. Trish adjusted her eating habits, and her daughters followed suit. Trish and Shelley began to "power walk" together thirty minutes a day. Both grew thinner; both grew closer. And before long, Shelley began to smile again.

Over the next few months, the braces came off. Contact lens went in. Wardrobe changes included new clothes that offered both fit and fashion. Trish watched with parental pride as Shelley's weight continued to fall, her confidence continued to rise, and her social calendar began to fill. Finally, her newfound friends got to meet the Shelley her mom knew was hiding within her all the time. Trish sees a lot less of Shelley these days (excuse the pun)—but she couldn't be happier.

Balance. That's the lesson to be learned *and* taught. Suggesting that appearance doesn't matter is untrue; suggesting that appearance matters most is unhealthy. As parents we need to help our kids do the best they can with what they've got. Teaching them to put their best foot forward is smart . . . making sure their shoes are shined is genius!

3

THE LIE
Life Is Fair

I UNDERSTAND THAT LIFE ISN'T FAIR,
BUT WHY COULDN'T IT JUST ONCE BE UNFAIR IN MY FAVOR?
Christy Murphy

I t seemed as though sixteen-year-old Jonathan had everything going for him . . . except his attitude. At school A's came easy. On the court, baskets came easy. At work, life was made easy—mostly because Jonathan was the boss's son. Maybe that's why none of his friends and few of his family could understand why Jonathan complained at every corner.

At school Jonathan frequently objected when students were given second chances or makeup exams—"Not fair!" On the court he constantly confronted referees when they missed a foul or made a mistake—"Not right!" At the supper table he regularly protested when his slice of pizza or piece of pie was smaller than the rest—"Not equal!" Overall, his attitude was "not good," and growing worse.

When asked why he whined so much at school, at games, and at home, Jonathan said, "Because it's not fair. Ever since I was young, my mom told me to treat people fair. Ever since

I started playing sports, my dad told me to play fair. If I'm fair with other people, they ought to be fair with me."

In a perfect world, Jonathan's right.
Everything's supposed to be fair.

When the Good Times Don't Roll

The list is endless. The stories are ruthless. The tears are countless:

Katilyn was a playful four-year-old, living in Duncan, British Columbia. On February 28, 1997, she had a seizure while at preschool. At first the doctors told her parents she'd be OK. She won't be. A subsequent series of medical exams revealed that Katilyn has Batten disease, a rare and incurable disorder that will fossilize her muscles . . . until she suffocates. Her parents live with the heartache of this discovery and the pain that comes from watching their child die. Meanwhile, in the house next door the neighbors are delirious with joy. They just won $600,000 in the lottery.[1]

Aleia Anderson was a gifted high-school junior from West Chicago, Illinois, who volunteered to participate in the Students Against Destructive Decisions (SADD) awareness program at her school. Hoping to educate her fellow classmates about the deadly consequences of drinking and driving, she was gratified to know that her efforts would make a difference in many young lives. Unfortunately, she was killed by a drunk driver less than a year later. She never saw her seventeenth birthday.[2]

In 1984 in Winston-Salem, North Carolina, nineteen-year-old Darryl Hunt was convicted of brutally beating, raping, and murdering twenty-five-year-old Deborah Sykes. On Christmas

Eve, 2003, he was released from prison after his attorneys successfully produced misplaced evidence and DNA tests that proved him innocent of the crime for which he was convicted. While Darryl is thankful to be free, his release came nineteen years after he was wrongfully imprisoned.[3]

Doug and Evan were elated with the birth of their first baby. During the delivery, however, Evan was given two units of blood from a supply that later tested positive for HIV. Mother and baby tested positive too. Doug's daughter lived two years and two months; his wife died shortly thereafter. Following the funerals, Doug continued his studies—to become a minister.[4]

We want to believe that justice is like gravity. It doesn't matter whether you live in Minneapolis or Miami, whether you're rich or poor, educated or illiterate, soldier or citizen—gravity makes sure that things always fall down, not up. Unfortunately, we live in a world where justice sometimes falls the wrong way:

- Olympic athlete is accidentally tripped from behind. Not fair!

- Boss's son is promoted; you're demoted. Not fair!

- Teenager aborts her unborn; you can't conceive. Not fair!

- Your younger sister is a size 2; you're a size 12. Really not fair!

The headline reads: "Drug Dealer Set Free on Legal Technicality." A few lines down, eight words drive the knife deeper: ". . . returned home to his mansion in a limousine." I live in a bungalow. My Durango, with 185,340 miles on it, sits in the driveway. Not fair!

When Wrongs Aren't Made Right

Sometimes a wrong can be made right. An injustice can be reversed. In other cases, by the time you get to the station, the train's already left.

That was the case for Lena Baker, who was tried and convicted for the murder of a man named E. B. Knight. During her trial, Lena testified that she shot Knight in self-defense when he raised a metal bar to strike her. Her jury was all-white and all-male. Lena was black. She went to prison.

In August 2005, injustice was reversed, and Lena was granted an unconditional pardon. The Georgia Board of Pardons read a proclamation admitting it had made a "grievous error." Unfortunately, her clemency came too late—sixty years too late. Lena Baker had been put to death in the state's electric chair in 1945 at the age of forty-four.[5]

We want to believe that life is fair so we can have peace for today and confidence for tomorrow. If life were fair, husbands would pick up one piece of clothing for every one piece dropped. Kids would put one toy back on the shelf for every one toy taken off. Academic grades would be based as much on effort as on aptitude. Grocery lines would proceed at the exact same rate, and all shopping carts would have four wheels that point in the same direction. Good people would be rewarded; bad people would be punished.

**If we were in charge,
that's the way the world would work, anyway.**

When it doesn't, we shake our heads, wring our hands, and look the other way. Justice takes a back seat to chance. Our foundation is shaken; our feet are on shifting sand. To help make sense of our situation, we purchase a fleet of best-selling books:

- *When Bad Things Happen to Good People*
- *When Bad Things Happen to Good Managers*
- *When Bad Things Happen to Good Marriages*
- *When Bad Grammar Happens to Good Writers*
- *When Bad Putts Happen to Good Golfers*

And my personal favorite:

- *When Bad Children Happen to Good Parents*

TRUTH OR CONSEQUENCES

The truth is that while we want life to be fair, it isn't. Because life's not fair, bad things happen to good people, and good things happen to bad people. We protest, we picket, we parade, but that's the way it is. We can't change it.

Suggesting to our kids that life is fair simply isn't fair—to them or to us. It sets them up to be disappointed; it sets us up to be dishonest. They deserve better, and so do we.

THE TRUTH

Life's not fair. It never has been, and it never will be. The bad news is, it will only be fair some of the time. The good news is . . . the same as the bad news.

Before you call your congressman to complain, here's something to think about: If life were fair, every time we exceeded the speed limit, we'd get ticketed. Every time we made a mistake at work, we'd be reprimanded. Every time we underreported our income or overreported our deductions, the IRS would catch us and fine us or jail us. Every time we told our kids a lie (even a well-intentioned one), our noses would grow a little longer. Now let me ask you: Do you still want life to be fair? All the time? Every day? For everybody?

Every coin has two sides. If life's not fair, then theoretically there will be times when you and I won't get what we deserve; we'll get what we desire. We deserve punishment; we'll receive pardon. We deserve failure; we'll receive fortune.

Despite my pathetic swing, sometimes the golf ball goes straight. Despite my choice not to study in college, sometimes my guess of C on a multiple-choice question was right. Despite the fifty other people in the room playing the same game, sometimes the numbers on my card line up, and I got to yell, "Bingo!" These kinds of good things may be more fluke than formula, but they *do* happen. Life may not be fair, but sometimes it does go our way.

Take Louis Daniels, for example. Louis is a college student attending Yale University. He's not the son of an elite blue-blooded father. He's not even the son of a hard-working, blue-collar father. Daniel spent most of his teenage years homeless, living in an assortment of shelters and motels. During his senior year in high school, he lived with his seven brothers and sisters at the Onesti Motel, located on a conjested stretch of the Jericho Turnpike in Huntington, New York. He spent most of his time studying on a mattress wedged in the corner above the motel's boiler room.

Daniel did so well with his schoolwork that he received a full-ride scholarship to the same school that has produced every American president since 1989. While going to school, Daniel lives a life of poverty among the privileged. He works three jobs: as a clerk, a tutor, and a member of the school custodial crew. Daniel earns thirteen dollars an hour cleaning dorm rooms, sweeping floors, washing windows, and wiping down desks—the same desks he sits in during class.

While being interviewed by a reporter, Daniel walked by a homeless man wearing a green wool sweater that was way too warm for an 80-degree day in June.

"Hey man, trying to get to Hartford. Can you spare a buck?" the homeless man asked, shaking a white Styrofoam cup that jingled with change.

"Here you go," said Daniel, plucking a dollar from his black wallet. "Peace."

You see, Daniel could relate. Others on the Corinthian-columned campus simply walked by.[6] Here's what Daniel knew to do that they didn't:

> When life is fair, thank God.
> When life isn't fair, thank God.

Responding to Injustice

I'm not suggesting that we roll over and play dead when life isn't fair. Sometimes we need to take action. In fact, let me encourage you to practice four responses to injustice (and teach them to your kids):

1. *Speak up if you're ever overcharged, mistreated, or unjustly unemployed* because you're a woman, a senior citizen, or

a minority. Such practices are not only unfair, they're illegal. Report them.

2. *Shut up if someone gets a bigger scoop of ice cream than you do.* There are limitless cases of serious injustice in this world to confront and correct; this is not one of them.

3. *Step up by doing the best you can with what you have.* Resist the temptation to cry "foul." In most cases the referee didn't see what happened, and half the people in the stands don't care anyway. When you find yourself on the short end of the stick, accept it, adjust to it, learn from it, and move on.

4. *Stand up and do the right thing, regardless of the cost*—simply because it's the right thing to do. You will live beyond the hardship, but you will remember how you handled it forever. It's bad enough that you were injured by the injustice; it would be worse if you lost your integrity as a result.

All four of these suggestions are good for parents to preach, and even better for parents to practice. Our kids are watching us. They're taking notes when injustice falls on Mom and Dad's doorstep. Be careful what you say. Be careful what you do. Model the behavior today that you desire to see in your children tomorrow.

In the meantime try this: after supper slice a pie unevenly and give each of your kids a different-sized piece for dessert. Once the cries of "It's not fair!" die down from those who received the smaller slices, tell them, "In life, some days you will get more than you deserve, and some days you will get less. The truth is, the world's not fair. Be thankful when you're helped. Be thoughtful when you're harmed."

Then remind your kids that 26,000 people around the world (mostly children) will die of starvation tonight . . . because they got none.

When Jonathan's parents realized that his endless whining at school, on the court, and at home was caused by his belief that life is fair, they asked him, "When was the last time you guessed correctly on a test question—and admitted to your teacher it was a guess?"

He was silent.

"When was the last time you committed a foul in basketball—and reported it to the referee?"

Silence again.

"When was the last time you drove over the speed limit—and notified the police?"

More silence.

Then they asked, "Do you still want the world to be fair?"

Jonathan stopped complaining.

4

THE LIE
It's the Thought That Counts

. . . AS LONG AS YOU'RE THINKING OF ME WHILE STANDING IN FRONT
OF THE JEWELRY COUNTER AT NEIMAN'S
WITH YOUR CHECKBOOK OPEN.

There was never any question that he loved her. Ang and Mary had been married for over fifty-five years. Throughout that time Ang provided for his wife in every way he could: nice car, nice clothes, nice kids, nice community. Ang was a blue-collar worker who labored with his hands, not his head. His job was a calling, not just a career. He was devoted to his wife, loyal to his family, and committed to his faith. Faults were hard to find—except one.

When Mary died at the age of eighty-six, the death certificate stated that she died as a result of kidney failure. Those who knew her best, though, would tell you that she died from a different disorder: a broken heart. Her kidneys may have taken her life, but a broken heart took her spirit long before.

Was Ang adulterous? Abusive? Alcoholic? Actually, he was much worse. He was actionless. Each Christmas, presents filled the room. The kids had a heyday. Mom had a heartache. Mary knew it was coming. The scene was repeated year after year. When all the gifts were opened, one present remained under the tree. It couldn't be avoided. It was for her.

Her anguish was not over the gift but the giver. The note read, "To Mary, from Ang." But the handwriting was obviously that of a minor, not a man. Once again Ang's daughter had come to his rescue. Once again she had purchased a present for her mom that was meant to look like it was from her dad. Notice I said "once again." This was not the first time, nor would it be the last. She knew that her father's good intentions to buy her a gift would not turn into action. Her father would provide for her mother in every area of life except one: her heart.

Ang's rationale? *I intended to get her a gift this year, but then I realized that she knows better what she wants.* Mary's rationalization? *At least he thought about getting me a gift, so it's OK; it's the thought that counts.*

They were both wrong.

Their kids were watching—and taking notes. On the tablets of their hearts that day, they wrote:

1. For some people, good intentions are the same as good actions.

2. For some people, it's OK if others make up for someone's shortcomings.

3. For some people, it's OK if this happens time and time again.

4. Our mother is one of those people.

5. There are probably more like her who think the same.

Mary's heart was broken because Ang's hands were always empty. Not just at Christmas, but at every birthday, Mother's Day, Valentine's Day, and wedding anniversary. It wouldn't have taken much to quench her thirst to feel "special." Any little trinket—made or purchased—would have sufficed. Instead, she continuously uttered seven words to hide her heartache: "That's OK; it's the thought that counts." Unfortunately, these words not only excused the behavior of her husband, but they also formed a belief in the hearts of her kids—a belief that would influence *their* behavior as well.

The Road Paved with Good Intentions

Those seven words, *That's OK; it's the thought that counts*, are often pressed into service as a charitable excuse for failure. They are spoken by the crushed and the compliant. They are designed to pardon rather than to penalize. They are words that every repentant criminal longs to hear from the judge just before sentencing.

Unfortunately, they are words that kids not only hear but learn to repeat.

Most people would describe Emily as a bright and busy sixteen-year-old. She's also very observant. While growing up, Emily often heard the saying, "It's the thought that counts." Her mother said it, excusing the behavior of her father when he came home with only a card for their anniversary one year and a wilted bouquet from the drugstore the next. Her father said it, excusing the behavior of his brother when Uncle Larry missed Emily's birthday year after year but sent a card with some cash tucked inside.

That's why her parents shouldn't have been surprised to hear those same words roll off Emily's lips after she hung up the phone with her good friend Ally. There had been a change of plans—and like the adults before her, Emily had the rationale to justify it. Ally's birthday was around the corner, and Emily had thought about taking her friend out to dinner . . . but she'd already spent too much of her allowance that week. She had thought about making Ally a special frame to hold a picture of the two of them . . . but she'd gotten too busy. She had thought about buying Ally that new top from Hollister that she knew Ally really wanted . . . but the store was across town and Emily had run out of time.

Finally, Emily had decided to give Ally a gift certificate from a store down the street. Emily's parents listened as their daughter told her friend that she would drop the certificate by her house the next day. Then Emily hung up the phone, saw the concerned look on her parents' faces, and said, "That's OK; it's the thought that counts."

Ally's heart was broken. Their friendship was weakened. Emily's parents were shaken. *Where would she get that idea?* they wondered.

Taking Matters into Their Own Hands

Frankly, it's common ground for therapists. We hear it over and over. We see it time and time again. Different variations—same underlying distortion: "It's the thought that counts." Many still believe it, but at least three patients I remember decided to confront it. This is what they had to say:

The first year we were married, my husband bought me a really expensive barbeque for my birthday. Nice gift, right? Actually, it turned out OK, because the following Christmas

I bought him a beautiful diamond tennis bracelet. He got the point!

Debbie

On our fifth anniversary my ex-husband gave me a card from the grocery store that read, 'You're so cute, you're a hoot,' with a twenty-dollar gift certificate tucked inside. Maybe that's why he's my ex-husband!

Sharon

The worst gift I ever got for Valentine's Day was radial tires for the car. He thought I'd be ecstatic because they were Michelins!

Kimberly

We may have the best of intentions, but if we don't make the effort to say "I love you" or "I appreciate you" in a way that is meaningful to the other person, "good intentions" just won't cut it. The fact is, there are many ways to say "I love you." My friend and best-selling author Gary Chapman has identified five "love languages" that we can use to express feelings of affection for one another:

- Gift giving

- Physical touch

- Words of affirmation

- Spending quality time together

- Acts of service[1]

In case you didn't notice, "good intentions" didn't make the list.

As Chapman says over and over in his book *The Five Love Languages*, expressing love in a language that the other person doesn't understand or appreciate is like speaking a foreign language. While I may think it's romantic for me to make my wife barbequed ribs on the grill for dinner, Jenni would prefer I make something else: a dinner reservation! Jenni's love language is clear; she doesn't care where I take her, as long as I do the planning, the parking, and the paying.

No matter what love language we choose, it has to be spoken or acted upon in order to be heard. Merely thinking about it leaves a lot to be desired—and a lot to be discussed. While theory has it that we should look past the gift and see the giver, the truth is that most of us see the giver through the gift. Love is what love does . . . or doesn't.

It's not about the price; sometimes it's about the presentation. One mom recently told me that her family was going through a tough time. Money was tight. They were burdened by debt and deficit. It seemed that just about the time they made enough money to make ends meet, somebody moved the ends.

So with her birthday on the doorstep, her kids got creative. Her oldest son gave her lilacs—her favorite flower. He picked them from a bush in the yard. Her youngest son followed suit by giving her a bouquet of everything blooming, from daffodils to dandelions. Her six-year-old daughter offered her a favorite doll to sleep with for an entire year. Isn't that neat? On the other hand, her husband came home with empty hands and hollow excuses. That night the kids slept well . . . while the dad slept on the couch!

In this world many people dream, but few people deliver.

Each of us must decide which group we're going to be part of—not only in our homes, but in our workplaces, our churches, and our communities. In case you haven't noticed, there is a short distance between "good intentions" and "good-bye." For example:

- Try telling your supervisor, "I planned on getting that report to you yesterday, but . . ."

- Or your patient, "I was going to check your x-rays, but . . ."

- Or the police officer, "I intended to buckle my seat belt, but . . ."

- Or the IRS, "I thought about filing a return last year, but . . ."

I think you get the idea.

TRUTH OR CONSEQUENCES

As parents we need to make sure our kids don't get caught in the "good intentions" trap. We need to observe their behavior and ask: Do they follow through with their dreams, desires, and intentions? Or do they stop at a thought and assume they get brownie points for simply thinking it? Our kids need to understand that anyone can have good intentions; the rewards, however, go to those who actually run the race, not the ones who think about it.

Will they miss the mark sometimes? Of course. We all do—children, parents, even presidents. We make an effort, but it's not appreciated. We use the wrong love language. But going for the mark and missing it is better than not going for it at all. We've said it before: actions speak louder than words. It's time to say it again. Our kids need to know the truth.

THE TRUTH

It is the thought that counts . . . as long as it's followed by action.

If you notice a consistent gap between your children's intentions and their actions—between their thoughts and their follow-through—then let me make the following suggestions:

1. *Make "outcome" the criteria for reward or reprimand.* Like it or not, we live in a world that is "results driven"—in school, at work, and at home. Good intentions are great, but kids need to learn to follow through with action. Thinking about doing something is a good start, but a poor outcome. When you survey an outcome with your kids, stick to the facts. What happened? What was the result?

2. *Determine why your children's behavior is falling short of their intentions.* The two most common reasons? Laziness and overcommitment. Laziness needs to be challenged; overcommitment needs to be changed. Setting realistic goals is the first step to accomplishing those goals and achieving success in the process. If your kids are overly optimistic about what they think they can accomplish within a finite period of time, be the voice of reason and help them balance their goals realistically.

3. *Major on action; minor on intention.* Since behavior that's rewarded is repeated, notice when a child does something right, and recognize it with words: "Brandon, I noticed that you put the milk back in the refrigerator after breakfast, and I really appreciate it. It sure helps Mom a lot when you clean up, and I just wanted to thank you." Set target behaviors for your children to accomplish, and respond with progressive rewards. Praise, payment, and privileges all work to increase the frequency of actions you want to see practiced, not just pondered.

4. *Never respond to your children with "That's OK; it's the thought that counts."* When you do, you reinforce laziness, carelessness, and thoughtlessness in your kids. Intention replaces action. Meditation replaces motion. And your nose grows a little bit longer. Instead, explain to your kids that positive thoughts and good intentions are great— but they won't get them anywhere if they're never acted upon. In basketball, points don't go on the scoreboard until the ball goes through the hoop. Nobody has ever scored a point by merely thinking about it!

Now it's time for me to come clean. I learned this truth the hard way. I saw it lived out before me. Remember Ang and Mary from the beginning of the chapter? She died with a broken heart because she lived with a broken belief. Ang meant well, but he did little. They both believed the lie that "it's the thought that counts." Well, I knew Ang and Mary by different names . . . they were my mom and dad.

5

THE LIE

It Doesn't Matter Whether
You Win or Lose —
It's How You Play the Game

IF WINNING DOESN'T MATTER,
THEN WHY DOES EVERYONE KEEP SCORE?

Brandon was seven the first time he heard the words. Minutes earlier the game had ended, and the outcome had been recorded. His team had lost the Carlisle Soccer championship game 8-1. They had scored one goal in forty minutes—and that was only because a defender from the other team accidentally kicked the ball off one of his teammates and it ricocheted into their net.

On the way home Brandon's parents had his undivided attention—after all, he was buckled in the backseat. Attempting to provide comfort as well as promote character, they told him, "Brandon, it doesn't matter whether you win or lose, it's how you play the game."

It wouldn't be the last time he heard that phrase. He heard it after most baseball games when he was eight, most basketball games when he was nine, and most peewee football games when he was ten, eleven, and twelve. Most of the time he heard it following a losing game, a losing season, or a losing effort.

It provided little consolation—and even less motivation.

At first the words were like being offered a ribbon for participation while the rest got trophies for prevailing. But over time, Brandon learned to embrace the words rather than resent them. He heard them so often that they didn't just shape his character, they defined it. By fourteen, Brandon learned how to lose—graciously, readily, willingly.

Over time, losing came easy. Over time Brandon lost his will to win. Over time Brandon's parents realized they had a more difficult challenge before them: helping their son develop the courage to compete.

From Losers to Winners

They were perpetual losers. The stands were deserted, the press was brutal, and the future looked bleak. Few wanted to watch, and even fewer wanted to play for a team that won only one game the entire season.

The date was 1957.

Fast forward to December 31, 1961. This same team won the NFL championship game by a score of 37-0 before a sold-out stadium of enthusiastic fans. Over the next six years they went on to dominate the league by winning six division titles, five NFL championships, and two Super Bowls. In less than ten years after that dismal 1957 season, they had become the measuring stick by which all other teams were judged.

What made the difference between disappointment and domination? One man. A coach who told his players, "Winning isn't everything—it's the only thing." His name: Vince Lombardi. His team: the Green Bay Packers. Like Charles Schwab, when Lombardi spoke, his players listened.

He taught the game from his heart. His lessons were forged from hardship. His practices were unrelenting. The field was a battleground. The team members practiced like they played and played like they practiced. For these professional athletes life was defined by fire, not favor. Lombardi told his players:

> Winning is not a sometime thing; it's an all-the-time thing. You don't win once in a while; you don't do things right once in a while; you do them right all the time. Winning is a habit. Unfortunately, so is losing.
>
> There is no room for second place. There is only one place in my game, and that's first place. I have finished second twice in my time at Green Bay, and I don't ever want to finish second again. . . . It is and always has been an American zeal to be first in anything we do, and to win, and to win, and to win.[1]

So impacted was the game of football by Lombardi's life and legend, that the NFL commissioned Tiffany & Co. to handcraft a trophy of sterling silver in his honor. Standing twenty-two inches tall, it's called the Vince Lombardi Trophy, and it's considered the NFL's most prestigious award. It's traditionally given by the Commissioner of Football to the owner of the winning team immediately following the Super Bowl.

It's a fact of American life:

The winning team is offered congratulations.
The losing team is offered condolences.

Our Winning Ways

America is obsessed with winning. From school grades to game shows, contestants (other than William Hung on *American*

Idol) will do anything to avoid having the word *loser* stamped on their foreheads. After all, there's big money in winning.

On November 19, 1999, a thirty-one-year-old IRS employee from Hamden, Connecticut, answered "Richard Nixon" when asked, "Who was the only U.S. President to appear on TV's *Laugh In*?" John Carpenter's "final answer" made him America's first millionaire on the popular television program *Who Wants to Be a Millionaire*. His prize paled in comparison to the $2.18 million Dr. Kevin Olmstead won on April 10, 2001, on the same show. After stating correctly that Igor Sikorsky invented the first mass-produced helicopter, he became the nation's twelfth million-dollar winner and the first game-show multimillionaire.

Then there was Rick Hess—another *Millionaire* contestant. Remember him? No? That's because his TV airtime amounted to two minutes, not two programs. Rick didn't get to the winner's circle because he never made it past Regis Philbin's fourth question. Like most game-show losers, he was escorted out the side door with a couple of complimentary parting gifts: a set of American Tourister luggage and a Bissell sweeper.

Not exactly what he had in mind.

You see, winning matters. In every contest there's the winner—and then there's everyone else. Nowadays the person who has the toughest time staying in college is the coach of a losing football team.

Think back to the 2004 Olympic Games in Greece, and contrast the happiness of Carly Patterson to the heartache of Stephon Marbury. Their faces at the closing ceremonies said it all. One beamed with ecstasy; the other was burdened with agony. One athlete returned home with gold, the other with gloom. Why? Because someone was keeping score.

Carly Patterson is the sixteen-year-old gymnast who dazzled the judges and won a gold medal for the United States in the Women's All-Round competition—a feat that hadn't been accomplished by an American female since Mary Lou Retton's performance twenty years earlier. Patterson won by only 0.176 of a point. Her future never looked brighter.

Stephon Marbury, on the other hand, was the professional basketball player who played point guard for the U.S. Men's Olympic basketball team. Before the Games, Marbury told ABC News correspondent Chris Bury that it's all about the gold—"for me, that's how I feel . . . nothing else will do."[2] Certainly, the Olympic cards were stacked in the Americans' favor. Only two U.S. Olympic basketball teams had ever returned home without a gold medal. Their overall record of 109 wins and 2 losses included winning their last twenty-five games in a row. The 2000 Olympic championship game had been close, but the Americans, as expected, had pulled it out. Afterward all-star point guard Jason Kidd admitted, "[If we had lost,] about 12 guys would have had to change their identities."[3]

Marbury and his 2004 Olympic teammates were ready to defend their gold medal. But on August 15, 2004, they got an Olympic wake-up call. They lost their opening game to Puerto Rico by nineteen points. Two losses later they found themselves dueling with Lithuania for third place. Fortunately, when the final buzzer sounded, the Americans were up by eight points. They won the game but lost the war. The players left the court after shaking hands; the fans left the building after shaking their heads.

Welcome to the bronze age.

Keeping Score

The scoreboard that hangs above the Dallas Mavericks basketball court is an eight-sided, 360-degree electronic message machine that cost $1.6 million. Why would a basketball team spend so much money for a scoreboard? Because they keep score.

Everywhere you turn these days, someone's got a clipboard in hand, recording the numbers. Keeping score.

Ask Hubert Humphrey, George McGovern, Walter Mondale, Michael Dukakis, and Bob Dole if the score means anything. Ask Al Gore if 533 votes in Florida mean anything to him.

Ask the unemployed investment broker who recommended buying stock in Winn-Dixie, Eastman Kodak, Rubbermaid, and Qwest Communications in 2003 if the numbers matter. The value of those four stocks dropped 38.2 percent, 25.5 percent, 24.4 percent, and 24.2 percent respectively.

Ask twelve-year-old Mark Corey if scores mean anything to him. According to his teachers, he'll be repeating the sixth grade next year at Chedoke Elementary School because his grades weren't good enough to pass.

Ask Kanoelani Gibson if scores mean anything to her. As Miss Hawaii, she lost the crown, the sash, and the cash (a $50,000 scholarship) to Miss Florida, Erica Dunlap, in the 2004 Miss America Pageant. According to the judges, Miss Florida had the higher score.

Ask your doctor if the numbers on your medical chart in the weight, blood pressure, and cholesterol columns mean anything to him (and to you). I think you get the idea.

TRUTH OR CONSEQUENCES

Of course, numbers, votes, and scores aren't everything.

The year was 1976. The place was the Olympic Stadium in Montreal, Canada. Twenty-two-year-old Mike Shine had just run the best race of his career in the 400-meter hurdles. He was ecstatic. The problem was, a twenty-year-old unknown sprinter from Morehouse College ran 1.05 seconds faster. His name was Edwin Moses.

Following the race, it was Shine who celebrated most. He ran with Moses for a victory lap, but for Mike Shine the run was more a dance for joy. Celebrate second place? Maybe he didn't get the memo: fame and fortune go to the well-accomplished, not the well-intentioned.

Sure enough, Edwin Moses did well. He became a man of great influence and greater affluence. His picture greeted us at the breakfast table on the front of the Wheaties box. He was recognized as one of the greatest one hundred athletes of the twentieth century. His plate was filled with commercial endorsements and speaking engagements.

When Shine returned home to Youngsville, Pennsylvania, the town held an honorary parade. A photo studio even shot his portrait free of charge. Today it hangs in the local high-school hallway. Thirty years after the race Mike Shine works in a cheese factory in Illinois.

Shine may not have come in first, but he was still a winner. In a 2004 interview on ABC's *Nightline*, Shine said he has no regrets. He ran his race. He did his best. He came in just one second slower than Edwin Moses. *One second.* As a result his face never graced the cover of a Wheaties box.

Mike said that's OK . . . he doesn't like Wheaties anyway.[4]

As Shine's example shows, not all the spoils of competition go to the victor. Competition develops character as much as it determines champions. Unfortunately, character is developed more by trials than by triumphs. Some of the most important lessons in life are learned when kids on the sidelines are watching their opponents on the podium. Attributes like discipline, integrity, sportsmanship, honesty, and teamwork are forged on the playing field, win or lose. Any coach worth his whistle will teach his players to respect their opponents and revere their referees, whatever the scoreboard says.

There's no question about it: character counts. How our children play the game matters. It matters to everyone who's smart enough to look past the scoreboard, and that should include parents. It definitely includes God. The truth is, kids who graduate from high school with an athletic scholarship or a perfect SAT score may get into a topnotch college, but if they're not "kids of character," their lack of integrity, honesty, and reliability will plunge their progress faster than a kite without wind.

Nevertheless, we miss the mark if we tell our children that the score doesn't matter. It does. On the court, those with the most points move on; those with the least move over. In the classroom, those with the highest grades succeed; those with the lowest, stumble. On the car lot, those with the most sales climb the corporate ladder; those with the least are shown the back door. There's no getting around it: everywhere our kids go, there will be somebody keeping score. Our children will forever be dealing with report cards, scoreboards, stop watches, and performance evaluations. That's life. They need to expect it—and they need to be prepared for it.

THE TRUTH

Winning isn't everything—but it does matter. People keep score for a reason.

Let me make one thing clear: winning doesn't equal worth. Kids need to know that their parents love them and value them whether they win or lose. They don't have to compete for our love—or for God's, for that matter. Their value lies in who they are, not what they do.

At the same time, there's nothing wrong with winning. We live in a competitive world, and if our kids are going to compete, they might as well compete to win. The apostle Paul put it this way: "Do you not know that in a race all the runners run, but only one gets the prize? Run in such a way as to get the prize" (1 Corinthians 9:24 NIV).

Succeeding in life doesn't mean winning every race. The real prize that Paul was talking about is eternal, not earthly, but the principle remains the same. Our job as parents is to teach our kids how to compete in every race—and how to *complete* every race they run. How to win—*and* how to play the game.

With this in mind let me suggest ten simple rules that you can post on your refrigerator:

1. Never fear failure; fear bystanding.

2. Never play their game; instead, play yours.

3. Never compromise your integrity for a victory.

4. Never attempt to live up to their standards; exceed them.

5. Never set goals so small that God has no room to show up.

6. Never give up. Never give in. Never resign. Never concede.

7. Never leave the field without learning one lesson to apply to life.

8. Never begin a race without visualizing a winning outcome in your mind.

9. Never accept the belief that it's better to lose by default than to lose by defeat.

10. Never play the game without keeping one eye on the ball, one eye on your opponent, and one eye on the score!

Let me encourage you to display these rules, describe these rules, and demonstrate these rules in your own life. Your kids are watching. No matter what the competition, teach your kids to show class when they win and character when they lose. Show them by your own example.

If they give it their all, they may just turn out to be another Edwin Moses. If they give it their all but don't come in first, they may turn out to be another Mike Shine. Both are winners in my book.

So is Brandon.

Brandon's parents decided to reframe the messages they spoke to their son, which reformed the effort he made on the field. They let him know that while his character must always rule his conduct, if he was going to play football, he might as well play to win. They taught him to practice hard, play tough, and produce much. They told him that his worth wasn't determined by the scoreboard, but his future could be.

The college scouts on the sidelines agree.

Know why I'm so proud of Brandon? Because he goes to practice early and stays late. Nobody works harder or plays tougher. Brandon gives it his all—all the time, every play, sixty minutes a game. When he walks off the field, there's nothing left, and that's what makes him a winner.

I wish I could report that his team went undefeated last year. They didn't. Winning isn't everything . . . but ten out of ten people will tell you it's better than the alternative.

6

THE LIE

God Helps Those
Who Help Themselves

PRAY AS IF EVERYTHING DEPENDED UPON GOD.
WORK AS IF EVERYTHING DEPENDED UPON MAN.
Francis Cardinal Spellman

Aron Ralston is a good-looking twenty-seven-year-old outdoorsman who sees a mountain and wants to conquer it. To this point, he's stood on the summit of forty-nine of Colorado's 14,000-foot peaks. It hasn't been easy. At one point he had a brush with death when he was buried alive by an avalanche. Unfortunately, it wasn't his last close call.

At 9:30 in the morning on April 26, 2003, Aron gathered his supplies—drinking water, four candy bars, camera, CD player, climbing gear, and trusty pocketknife—and began what was supposed to be an eight-hour, thirteen-mile hike into the remote hills of Canyonlands National Park in Utah. Five hours later things went wrong. Terribly wrong.

**Aron found himself caught between a rock and a hard place.
Literally.**

While scaling a three-foot-wide slot canyon, an eight-hundred-pound chalkstone boulder shifted and pinned his right hand against the ravine wall. Over the next five days Aron tried everything to set himself free. Nothing worked. His food was depleted. His canteen was dry. His hope was dwindling. Then Aron did the unthinkable. Like an animal caught in a spring-loaded bear trap, he cut off his arm. Aron crafted a makeshift surgical kit from his supplies—and amputated his right forearm with the blunt blade of his three-inch pocketknife. The grisly operation took about an hour to complete.

"I was able to first snap the radius and then within another few minutes snap the ulna at the wrist. From there I had the knife out and applied the tourniquet and went to task," he told reporters later. Unfortunately, his ordeal didn't end with the surgery. After freeing himself from the boulder, he had to crawl through the narrow, winding canyon, rappel down a sixty-foot cliff, and walk six miles before finding two other hikers who called for medical help.

"I may never fully understand the spiritual aspects of what I experienced, but I will try," Aron said. "The source of the power I felt was the thoughts and prayers of many people, most of whom I will never know."[1] According to Aron, "prayer power" may have accounted for his willpower, but his relief came in his resolve to act. He told *Outside* magazine, "Maybe this is how I handled the pain. I was just happy to be taking action."[2]

Contrast the performance of Aron Ralston with the paralysis of Sal and Mable Mangano. Prior to the arrival of Hurricane Katrina in August 2005, New Orleans Mayor Ray Nagin ordered the residents of the city to evacuate. The largest and most powerful hurricane ever tracked by the National Hurricane Center was swelling in the Gulf of Mexico and heading straight for their city—a city that sits eight feet below sea level.

Sal and Mable Mangano owned St. Rita's Nursing Home in

St. Bernard Parish. Sixty residents—including the elderly and the immobile, the delicate and the disabled—counted on the Manganos to care for their needs. They were let down—horribly. According to Louisiana Attorney General Charles Foti Jr., the Manganos were offered buses to evacuate the residents of St. Rita's and had a contract with Acadian Ambulance Service to provide transportation in the event of an emergency. Neither was utilized.[3]

When the water began to subside, rescue workers searching the city for the wet and wounded discovered the inconceivable. More than thirty bodies were found at St. Rita's Nursing Home. All had drowned. Apparently, Sal and Mable believed that because the nursing home had been built on higher ground, it would be spared, just as it had in 1965 following the flood from Hurricane Betsy. They were so confident that God would preserve their one-story brick building that they invited relatives and staff to join them at the nursing home. Once the levy broke, it took twenty minutes for the water to reach the ceiling of the center. All was lost. Sal and Mable have been charged with thirty-four counts of negligent homicide.[4]

Whether you're the victim of a fallen rock or a rising tide, the question is, what are you going to do about the circumstances you're in?

Some will take matters into their own hands; some will place matters into God's hands. Both camps have reasons to believe they're doing things God's way. Which is correct? The answer is important—for us and for our kids.

I Know It's in There Somewhere

Most of us would commend Aron Ralston for his courageous action and condemn Sal and Mable Mangano for their shortsighted inaction. That's because we've been told that "God helps those who help themselves." In fact, according to pollster George Barna, 82 percent of us believe that the statement "God helps those who help themselves" is in the Bible. (Unfortunately, Barna also found that half of those surveyed believe that Sodom and Gomorrah were husband and wife!)[5]

The words may not be found in Scripture and printed in red, but they're in there somewhere. Right? They must be! "God helps those who help themselves" is not just the biblical way; it's the American way. We do our part and God does his. We plant the flowers and God grows them. We say our prayers and God answers them. That's the deal; that's the way the system works.

The truth is, "God helps those who help themselves" isn't found in Scripture—anywhere. Actually, the first to be credited with this axiom was Aesop, about five hundred years before Christ. In one of Aesop's Fables, the story goes like this:

> A waggoneer was once driving a heavy load along a very muddy way. He came to a part of the road where the wheels sank halfway into the mire, and the more the horses pulled, the deeper sank the wheels. So the wagoneer threw down his whip, knelt down, and prayed to Hercules: "Oh, Hercules, help me in my hour of distress." But Hercules appeared to him and said, "Man, don't sprawl there. Get up and put your shoulder to the wheel. *The gods help them that help themselves.*"[6]

Euripides, a Greek writer and philosopher who lived between 480 and 406 BC, said something similar: "Try first thyself, and after, call on God."[7] In the seventeenth century, George Herbert said, "Help thyself, and God will help thee."[8] But the most recent version—with the exact words we know today—can be traced to a book called *Poor Richard's Almanack*, published in 1736. The author? Benjamin Franklin.[9]

Franklin detested religious practices. But like many of his colonial colleagues in the flourishing city of Philadelphia, he believed that hard work warmed God's heart. So he wrote, "God helps those who help themselves."

Here are some other quotes attributed to Benjamin Franklin (along with their modern interpretation):

Franklin: "Never leave until tomorrow that which can be done today."

Today's version: Never do today what can be put off until tomorrow. Who knows? You might win the lottery, and then you can hire someone else to do it.

Franklin: "Early to bed, early to rise makes a man healthy, wealthy, and wise."

Today's version: Late to bed and late to rise means that you can watch Leno and sleep at your desk in the morning.

Franklin: "A penny saved is a penny earned."

Today's version: A penny saved is a penny wasted. Help the economy—go buy something! If you want to be really patriotic, buy two.

Franklin: "Never confuse motion with action."

Today's version: Actually, motion and action are both confusing. Just relax, sit back, and chill.

Franklin: "Well done is better than well said."

Today's version: "Well done" is how I order a steak. "Well said" is expressing the order in such a way that the waiter understands, and the cook gets it just right.

Wouldn't Ben be proud at how America has progressed?

Houston, We Have a Problem

Obviously, many of Franklin's principles have fallen by the wayside over the years. But "God helps those who help themselves" is one that has stuck. It may not be in the Bible, but parents have been telling this tale to their kids for generations. Taken at face value, it's a principle that promotes initiative, responsibility, and cooperation with the Creator. What could possibly be wrong with that? Not a thing.

Unfortunately, message sent isn't always message received.

I remember hearing a story about a regional airport in the Midwest that was temporarily shut down due to a severe winter snowstorm. Planes were forced to circle for hours as crewmen checked snow accumulations on the ground. Suddenly from the tower the crewmen heard, "This is an emergency . . . clear the runway!" Frantically, workers flooded onto the runway with every man and machine they could find, clearing the snow as fast a possible. Unfortunately, they found out too late that Flight 467 from San Diego was out of fuel and just seconds from an emergency landing. The message from the tower was to clear the runway of *people*—not snow.

Let's face it: message sent and message received are often two different messages. That's the problem with "God helps those who help themselves"—it's often miscommunicated (especially between parents and kids) and frequently misunderstood. It may be well-intended, but biblically speaking, it's not well-proven. It may be motivating, but it can also be misleading. Psychologically sound, but theologically skewed. Let's take a closer look.

Most parents recognize the importance of developing

"children of character." These kids will succeed in any setting because their actions are based on internal standards rather than external circumstances. They will do well in private schools, public schools, and home schools. Their behavior is determined by their character, not dictated by a parent, principal, or policeman.

On its surface, "God helps those who help themselves" facilitates this development. It encourages two important character traits: initiative and responsibility. Most of us want to develop these qualities in our kids—the same way our parents developed these qualities in us. The lesson we received from our parents was taught early and taught often. For most of us it went like this:

"Mom, how do you spell *conscientious?*"

Mom: "Try to sound it out."

"I can't. It's too hard."

Mom: "Then look it up in the dictionary."

"I can't look it up because I can't spell it. If I knew how to spell it, I wouldn't have to look it up in the first place."

Mom: "Honey, you just need to learn that *God helps those who help themselves.*"

The principle was purposeful, but was it truthful? The fact is, most of us discovered that if we doodled in the dictionary long enough, Mom would eventually come to the rescue. The implication was that God would do the same. While there's an element of truth in this belief, there's also an element of error. The apostle Paul made it clear that God is not a fan of those who want to doodle and then sit down for dinner. In 2 Thessalonians 3:10, Paul wrote, "If anyone will not work, neither let him eat."

Neither is God a fan of self-reliance. Time and time again

Scripture encourages personal responsibility but opposes self-reliance. The two may seem similar, but they're *not* the same thing; the first is to be encouraged; the latter is to be erased. When the good times roll, the responsible feel grateful; the self-reliant feel deserving. When times are tough, the responsible look up; the self-reliant look in. Solomon, the wisest man to ever live, wrote about self-reliance this way: "He who trusts in his own heart is a fool" (Proverbs 28:26). The self-reliant believe that "God helps those who help themselves" because, after all, he *needs* them. News flash: he doesn't.

God is also not a fan of those who think they can gain his favor by doing his work. *Quid pro quo* is a Latin term often used in legal settings that means "one thing in return for another." In the vernacular of our day it's like, "You scratch my back, and I'll scratch yours." Here's more late-breaking news: God doesn't need his back scratched. God's not obligated to help me hit the ball out of the park simply because I whisper a prayer while standing in the batter's box. He can't be manipulated and refuses to be obligated. God shows up sometimes simply because . . . he's God.

TRUTH OR CONSEQUENCES

Every soccer mom worth her minivan wants to develop the qualities of initiative, responsibility, and cooperation in her kids. These are the cornerstones of character that will pay dividends in the lives of her children long after her retirement funds run dry. So when we say, "God helps those who help themselves," our intentions may be honorable, but our theology is questionable. Consider these examples from the Bible:

- With their heels in the Red Sea and the Egyptians in their rear-view mirror, the Israelites had nowhere to turn, nowhere to hide, nowhere to run. God parted the Red Sea and made a way of escape. (see Exodus 14:13–30)

- With their faith in hand and flames at their feet, Shadrach, Meshach, and Abed-nego could do nothing to save themselves. They prayed and God sent an angel to deliver them from the fiery furnace. (see Daniel 3:1–30)

- With nothing more than the belief that God would be his protector, Daniel was directed into the lions' den, destined to be a bedtime snack for some very hungry cats. By morning the lions were more like pets than predators. (see Daniel 6:10–24)

- With funeral proceedings completed, there was nothing more for Mary and Martha to do except gather the relatives for moaning and macaroni salad. Then Jesus spoke into their brother's tomb, "Lazarus, come forth." Immediately there was life in his bones and breath in his lungs. (see John 11:1–4)

Each of these passages offers us an example of people who couldn't help themselves and saw God show up. Had they believed that "God helps those who help themselves," they would have tried different options, and God would have allowed different outcomes. The good news is, when they were incapable of helping themselves, God showed up. The even better news is that he can do the same for you and your kids.

THE TRUTH

God has a history of helping those who *can't* help themselves.

I'm reminded of the ninth-grade boy who was picked on and punched daily by an eleventh-grade terrorist who enjoyed humiliating his newfound target. To the tormentor, this was worth going to school for. To his target, this was reason to resign.

There was no solution. The torment took place when teachers were absent, and students were silent. To the 135-pound boy, facing this school-yard Goliath seemed senseless; his muscles were marginal, and his friends were invisible. If God helped those who helped themselves . . . this boy was doomed.

One Friday night in February he went tobogganing with his twenty-one-year-old sister, her fiancé, and his brother. Trudging to the top of Chedoke Hill and looking out over the snow-covered landscape, he could see forever. That's when he experienced his worst nightmare: the titan of terrorism was making his way up the hill, and a winter version of having sand kicked in his face was only moments from reality.

Harassed at school and soon to be embarrassed in the snow, he remembered his parents' words: "When your back is against the wall, don't look in, don't look out—instead, look up." Unable to help himself, he whispered prayers. But this situation looked as hopeless as a shepherd boy's facing a seasoned, armor-clad warrior with nothing but a sling.

Hmmm.

As the bully stepped forward to make fun of his prey, so did two others. Not teachers, not students, not friends—but family. In stepped his sister's twenty-three-year-old fiancé and his twenty-one-year-old brother. Words were spoken, coats were clenched, and promises were made: "If you touch him again, you'll deal with us. Got it? Now beat it."

That's it. This terrorist was tamed. Freedom was secured for not only a nighttime, but a lifetime . . . because the bully never touched *me* again. That's right, this is *my* story. I couldn't help myself, and God sent two angels to my rescue when I had nowhere else to turn. I just knew them as Bill and John.

As parents we need to tell our kids the truth: God tends to show up when there's nothing we can do to help ourselves. At the same time we need to teach our kids the value of personal responsibility without promoting self-reliance—and without promoting false ideas about how God wants to work in our lives. How? Let me offer the following suggestions:

1. *Teach your kids to refrain from asking God to do for them what they're perfectly capable of doing for themselves.* Laziness isn't an attribute that God admires; people don't either.

2. *Demonstrate to your kids that you will help them if they will make a real effort first.* Here are a few messages that are both healthy and helpful:

   - "Pick up all the toys you can; then I'll help you with the ones that may be too heavy for you."

   - "Sell as many Girl Scout cookies as you can; then I'll help you sell the rest."

- "Shovel as much snow as you can; then I'll help you shovel the rest."

3. *Teach your kids to remember and repeat: "God helps those who stop hurting themselves."* This rule applies to all areas of life—physical, emotional, and spiritual. For example, physically, we can't eat an endless supply of bonbons and baked goods and expect God to make us fit. Emotionally, we can't constantly duck personal responsibility and expect God to eliminate the consequences. Spiritually, we can't neglect spending time in prayer and Bible reading and expect God to keep us connected. Work with God, not against him.

4. *Teach your kids that they don't have to jump through spiritual hoops in order to merit God's favor or his friendship.* Tell them, "When your back is against the wall and there's nowhere left to turn, don't look in, and don't look around—look up. Conditions are just about right for God to show up."

By the way, now that we've uncovered one saying that most people think is penned in the pages of Scripture, here are some others to consider:

- "Cleanliness is next to godliness."

- "Spare the rod and spoil the child."

- "To thine own self be true."

- "This, too, shall pass."

- "God works in mysterious ways."

    You won't find them in the Bible either.

7

THE LIE
Love Will Last a Lifetime

MARRIAGE ISN'T SUPPOSED TO MAKE YOU HAPPY,
IT'S SUPPOSED TO MAKE YOU MARRIED.

Frank Pittman

Wedding bells are about to ring for Shane and Wendy. After a sixteen-month engagement they will be walking down the aisle at First Baptist Church on June 22 at five o'clock in the afternoon. For twenty-five-year-old Wendy and twenty-seven-year-old Shane, this will be their first trip down the aisle.

Both intend it to be their last.

Wendy will be wearing an ivory Signature Collection halter A-line gown with a satin skirt and beaded lace appliqués. Her elbow-length veil has matching beads and pearls. Shane will look impressive in a black three-button Oleg Cassini tuxedo with wing-collar shirt, champagne retro-paisley fullback vest, matching bow tie, and square-toe lace-up shoes. At the reception afterward, 178 people will join them as they dine and dance, and then Wendy and Shane will depart for their honeymoon. The events of the day will cost $26,800 . . . but other than Wendy's father, who's counting?[1]

On an average day in America, 6,200 couples will tie the marital knot. The largest number of weddings will take place in Las Vegas (329 to be specific).[2] Statistically, Shane and Wendy represent an average couple in many ways: age, length of engagement, first marriage, June wedding, number attending the reception, and price tag. Unfortunately, because they do represent an average couple in America, the National Center for Health Statistics says there's a 43 percent chance they won't make it to their fifteenth wedding anniversary.[3] In fact, of all first marriages that end in divorce, most do so only 3.4 years after the newlyweds say, "I do."[4]

Hmmm. Shane and Wendy think their love will last a lifetime. Where did they get that idea? Probably from their parents.

The Message Was in the Music

Remember Daryl and Toni Dragon? You may not know them by their given names, but if you're anywhere close to my age, you'll remember them as one of the most successful duos in modern pop music. They met in 1971. He was known as "Captain Keyboard," and in 1975 she became his first mate at the Silver Queen Wedding Chapel in Nevada. Together they recorded seven top-ten singles, five gold albums, six gold singles, two platinum albums, and one platinum single. Maybe you'll recognize their stage name: Captain & Tennille.

In 1975 the duo released a song written by Neil Sedaka and Howard Greenfield that debuted on Billboard's Hot 100 at Number 98 but soared to Number 1 nine weeks later. That tune earned Captain & Tennille a Grammy award for Record of the Year, and instant fame.[5] From my perspective it's the second worst song I've ever heard. The title says it all: "Love Will Keep Us Together." The message? Love is stronger than Super Glue. It can hold any twosome together.

It sounded good then. It sounds good now. But the question remains: is it true?

What's Love Got to Do with It?

I remember hearing a story about a couple—Helen and George— who threw a party to celebrate their fortieth anniversary. Soon after their family and friends departed, they got ready for bed.

"George, why did you marry me forty years ago?" Helen asked. Expecting to hear something romantic like, "Because I loved you," or "Because you were so beautiful, I just couldn't take my eyes off of you." She was startled when she heard, "Just stupid, I guess."

"That's not very encouraging," Helen said to her romantically challenged husband.

"Sure it is, honey. I hear about couples falling out of love all the time, but I've never once heard of anybody falling out of stupid."

Most of us have been led to believe that love is the glue that enables a marriage to stand the test of time—and even the test of torment. Remember the words you repeated after the minister?

"For better or for worse,
for richer or for poorer,
in sickness and in health,
for as long as we both shall live"?
No escape clause. No qualifiers. No disclaimers. No loopholes.

The fact is, according to John Crouch, executive director of Americans for Divorce Reform, there are a number of variables that significantly improve your chances for a lifelong marriage and lessen the odds of turning an "I do" into an "I don't." Unfortunately, love isn't one of them. Crouch's research shows that the likelihood of divorce is reduced:

- 30 percent if your annual income is over $50,000

- 24 percent if you refrain from having a baby before your first anniversary

- 24 percent if you're over twenty-five when you marry

- 14 percent if your parents remained married

- 14 percent if you are spiritually minded

- 13 percent if you attended college

Putting it all together, Crouch concludes that if you are a reasonably well-educated couple with an annual income of $50,000 or more, if you come from intact families and have similar religious values, and if you marry after you're both twenty-five and wait at least one year before having a baby, your chances of divorce are relatively small.[6] Did you notice? Not one mention of "love." Not one.

TRUTH OR CONSEQUENCES

"Do you love him?" That's a question every parent should ask a daughter who returns home from college wearing an engagement ring. Hearing her say yes is a feeling every parent should experience. But thinking this love will hold the two lovebirds together forever is a belief every parent should dispel.

According to the latest research, the top five characteristics that predict long-term marital success are:

1. Commitment to marriage

2. Loyalty to spouse

3. Strong moral values

4. Respect for spouse

5. Fidelity[7]

(Don't bother checking; "love" isn't in 6 through 10 either.)

The fact is, love is a feeling, relationships are work, and marriage is a commitment. Confuse these three, and we end up teaching our kids that marriage is "magical," and love is the wand that makes it happen. It isn't. If we find ourselves saying, "That's all that matters, dear—as long as you love each other," our noses grow a little bit longer.

THE TRUTH

Love can last a lifetime . . .
as long as it's coupled with commitment.

Both the test of time and the test of research prove that commitment, not love, is the cement that holds two people together through the wind, the rain, and the storms of marital life. Commitment is a decision that holds a marriage together, while love is a feeling that makes it worthwhile. Love may be the spark that gets the fire started, but commitment is the fuel that keeps it burning.

Just ask Betty in Cape May, New Jersey. Here's what she wrote to Dear Abby in February 2001:

> Dear Abby,
>
> Some months ago you printed a letter from a reader who was disturbed that the spark was gone from her marriage. I asked my husband whether the spark is gone from our eighteen-year marriage. His response: "A spark lasts only a second. It lights a fire. When the flame burns down, we are left with the hottest part of the fire, the embers, which burn the longest and keep the fire alive."[8]

Those embers represent commitment. Unfortunately, as Michael McManus, a longtime marriage advocate, has observed, "Today's marriages are built on a slippery slope of changing feelings and circumstances—rather than a rock of commitment."[9]

The Look of Love

Kids have a funny way of seeing things, sorting things, and saying things. If you want to get to the point on a subject, just ask someone under ten. Children see with their hearts as much as with their eyes. They don't know about being politically correct or academically credentialed. They haven't been corrupted by a statistics class, so they tell it like it is—the good, the bad, and the funny.

Some time ago a number of kids were asked about their perspectives on love. This is what they had to say:

Question: "What do most people do on a date?"

Mike, age ten: "On the first date they tell each other lies. That usually gets them interested enough to go on a second date."

Question: "When is it OK to kiss someone?"
Jim, age nine: "You should never kiss a girl unless you have enough money to buy her a ring and a VCR, 'cause she'll want to watch videos of the wedding."

Question: "What do looks have to do with falling in love?"
Gary, age seven: "Actually, they don't have much to do with it. Look at me. I'm handsome like anything, and I haven't got anyone to marry me yet."

Question: "How do you feel about falling in love?"
Courtney, age six: "Well, I'm generally in favor of it, as long as it doesn't happen when *Lion King* is on TV."

Question: "How do you know if two people are in love?"
Brad, age seven: "Well, people in love don't eat their food until it's cold. They just stare at each other."

Question: "How do you keep love alive?"
Eric, age eight: "Don't forget your wife's name. That would really mess things up."
Randy, age nine: "Be a good kisser. It might make your wife forget that you never take out the garbage."

Trust me, Randy, it won't matter!

Out of Tune

Where do kids get these ideas about love? From us. They're watching and they're listening—closely. The question is, what message are we sending? Is it a realistic message that will lead them into a fulfilling, committed, long-term marriage, or is it a "pie-in-the-sky" message that promises more than it can deliver?

Go ahead, admit it: we were lied to—in stereo. Captain & Tennille sang "Love will keep us together" in one ear, while the Beatles chanted, "All you need is love" in the other. Different music styles, same misguided message. Without thinking, most of us believed it, and many of us promoted it—either by our speech or by our silence. It's a message that makes for a best-selling song but a short-lived marriage.

Music styles have changed since then, but the message hasn't. Today's rappers and rock stars promote relationships without rings and sex without strings. Love (or, more accurately, lust) without commitment is still the mantra of the day. The message isn't new, but it's more powerful, more persistent, and more pornographic than ever.

As parents we must be the ones to tell our kids the truth. Love without commitment won't keep them together any more than bricks without cement will build a strong wall. If we lead them to believe that love alone will keep their car on the road (even when their relational, physical, spiritual, and financial wheels are falling off), then we're raising kids who are dreaming when they should be driving. *Beauty and the Beast* may be a great bedtime story of a love that overcomes the impossible, marries the improbable, and lives the inconceivable . . . but it's still a fairy tale that's hard to believe after you've kissed your kids goodnight and turned out the lights.

What *is* believable is that marriage can last a lifetime if it's built upon a firm foundation. Commitment is the centerpiece of that foundation, not love. Why? Commitment is a decision; love is an emotion. One is made by the head; the other is made by the heart. Love is a great feeling, but commitment is a great footing. That being the case, let me ask you: which do you want your kids to build a marriage upon—a feeling or a foundation?

I thought so!

So if your daughter returns home from college informing you that she's met "Mr. Right," or your son tells you he's thinking about asking his girlfriend the "big question," let me encourage you to ask one simple thing: "Why do you want to get married?" If they respond with "because we're in love" and nothing more, you have the responsibility to tell them they're about to take a marital ride with many more valleys than peaks. It's called a "marriage-go-round."

Want to help your kids avoid that scenario? Here are a few things you can teach them:

1. When it comes to marriage, they should look long . . . before they leap.

2. Time will tell the difference between love and lust. Make time their ally, not their enemy.

3. Someone running into a marriage is usually someone running away from something else: singleness. Walk, don't run, from that scenario.

4. Love can last a lifetime, if it's coupled with commitment—and prove it by example.

5. Choosing a divorce because love has "died" is like selling a car because it ran out of gas. Encourage them to get marital therapy and design the marriage they desire.

By the way, earlier I mentioned that I thought "Love Will Keep Us Together" by Captain & Tennille was the second worst song I'd ever heard. The worst? "Muskrat Love."

8

THE LIE

Leaders Are Born, Not Bred

HE'S A NATURAL-BORN LEADER!
Every father of a newborn son

Imagine reading the newspaper one morning and stumbling upon the following birth announcement:

Mr. and Mrs. Confidence are proud to announce the birth of their twelve-pound-nine-ounce son, Sampson. With his first robust cry, unbridled enthusiasm, and natural leadership skills, he was immediately registered with Dale Carnegie as a preschool motivational leader. Shortly after he arrived in the nursery, his parents were found reading to him from the book *Your Future as Leader of the Free World*.

Now imagine it's four years later. A one-way mirror separates the examined from the examiner. Like a scientist watching white mice in the lab, you find yourself rating, ranking, and recording. You may be out of sight, but you're not out of curiosity.

You're at Benjamin Bunny Preschool, and you're watching your four-year-old bundle of joy interact with his preschool peers. The class of fourteen toddlers is about to enjoy fifteen minutes of playtime before mealtime and naptime. At first the kids stampede through the room like wild mustangs let loose on the range. Each races to his or her favorite pastime—the chalkboard, the dollhouse, the bouncy balls. Then something interesting begins to happen. The biggest boy of the bunch starts to organize their playtime. Some kids he directs, some he dominates, some he drags. One by one, all of the kids—yours included—sit on the floor and listen to him like soldiers before their sergeant. They sit motionless, fearing his fury, desiring his favor. Soon they stand and begin to follow him as he marches around the playroom like Napoleon Bonaparte at Montenotte.

That's when the mother standing next to you says, "That's my son, Sampson. He's a natural-born leader."

Hmmm.

Now questions come as quickly as popcorn in a pressure cooker:

- "What does that make *my* son—a natural-born *follower?*"

- "Was his future as a follower determined at birth?"

- "Is he destined to be dominated by kids like Sampson for the rest of his life?"

- "What can I do to develop leadership skills in my kids that will last them a lifetime?"

The Look of Leadership

Leadership is influence. Whether a leader is a preschooler, a parent, or the president of the United States, he or she exercises leadership by influencing others at home, at school, at the office, and beyond. Truly effective leaders are priceless. No matter who they lead, no matter where they're going, no matter what their destination, leaders inspire us to move forward, travel faster, and go farther.

What exactly does a leader look like? A Washington think tank examined the history books and concluded that if you'd like to trade in your home office for the Oval Office, there are seven characteristics that will greatly increase your chances of becoming the president of the United States. After reviewing the records, they determined that most of America's forty-three presidents have been six feet tall, married, fathers, charismatic, promoters of a politically correct agenda, with a last name averaging six letters—and, of course, male.[1]

At least to this point.

If those are the traits we should look for in a leader, Agnes had none. Born on August 27, 1910, to an Albanian contractor and his wife, Agnes Gonxha Bojaxhiu never desired to be president of the United States, but she did end up being equally distinguished as a world leader. Standing less than five feet tall, she soared over her circumstances. She had no political power, no property, and few possessions. Yet she was honored on the world stage with a Templeton Award in 1973, the Albert Schweitzer International Award in 1975, the Nobel Peace Prize in 1979, and the Presidential Medal of Freedom in 1985. By the time she died on September 5, 1997, her passion, her piety, and her influence were responsible for creating 570 Missions of Charity on five continents. Over her lifetime, Agnes recruited 4,000 nuns and 100,000 lay volunteers to feed 500,000 families a day and care for 90,000 lepers a year. Who was this powerhouse of performance who led by service and sacrifice? Those who knew her best referred to her as the "Angel of Mercy." The rest of us knew her as Mother Teresa.[2]

Like Agnes, Arthur Currie didn't look much like a leader either. In fact, his large, pear-shaped body and chubby face gave many the impression of an undisciplined man. Psychologically, he didn't look much better. Currie was passed over by the military brass because of test results and personality profiles that showed him to be too sensitive, too trusting, and too detailed. Neither imaginative, insightful, nor inspirational, his superiors concluded that Arthur would make a good pencil pusher, not a pacesetter. It turned out, however, that nothing was further from the truth.

Promoted because of his performance on the field, General Arthur Currie led his men to Canada's greatest military success at Vimy Ridge in 1917. Although 10,602 soldiers were wounded and 3,598 were killed, Currie led his forces in an unbroken string of successes, defeating sixty-four enemy divisions. He never lost a single inch of ground, never lost a single piece of artillery, and never failed a single military assignment.[3]

Whether in the ministry like Mother Teresa or in the military like General Currie, leaders make a difference in this world. They may come from vastly different backgrounds and display vastly different personalities, yet most leadership experts agree that certain common characteristics account for their success. What the experts don't agree on is where those characteristics originate.

Are leaders born in the womb or bred in the world? Are leadership traits caught, or are they taught? Ask the experts these questions, and most will answer, "Yes."

Hmmm.

A Tale of Two Theories

Aristotle was the first to frame the belief that some men are born to lead, while others are born to be led. Like many of his day, he was convinced that leaders were made in the womb, not in the world. "Natural-born leaders" were the product of inborn traits passed down from generation to generation, like blue eyes and blond hair. No amount of education or experience could be sufficient to give leadership ability to someone who was not born with these inherited characteristics.

Naturally, the people who most readily agreed with Aristotle were the socially elite, the financially blessed, and the politically powerful. In typical self-serving manner, they believed that leadership was tied to birth order and family background. "We lead; you follow . . . any questions?" European monarchies maintained their authority with this belief and paired it with prearranged marriages among the ruling elite. There were no problems as long as an heir (and not a revolution) was born.

Centuries later the birth of psychology confirmed this popular line of thought about leaders. In the 1920s and 1930s, leadership research focused on identifying the traits that separated the chiefs from the Indians, the leaders from the followers. This "trait theory" assumed that certain physical, social, and personal traits were inherent in effective leaders and missing in others. Traits could be identified and then used to assist management in selecting the "right" people to lead the "rest" of the people. Leadership traits that focused on the physical included age, height, and appearance. Social traits included education, social skills, charm, popularity, and charisma. Personality traits included confidence, assertiveness, emotional stability, drive, flexibility, and initiative.

But what the new field of psychology first supported, later it sank. Scientific evidence designed to validate the trait theory came back contradictory and inconclusive. In 1948 Ralph Stogdill published a classic study that challenged the prevailing thought that innate traits predicted leadership success.[4] The famous "Stogdill Paper" sidelined most "born-based" leadership theories and kept them out of the classroom for decades.

It didn't take a rocket scientist to figure out that not all of the hand-me-down "leaders" were effective in leadership. Many were simply descendents with pass-me-down authority. Some succeeded, some stalled; and some, like the theory itself, just sank.

While most experts remained convinced that certain traits accounted for leadership success, the debate began to center on their origin: was it nurture or nature? Over time, the tide began to turn. Experts began to believe that many leadership traits could be imparted, not just inherited. The "bred theory" proposed that leadership could be taught from a textbook and perfected by practice. Before long this idea moved to the top of the leadership totem pole, and the "leadership training" business was birthed.

At the heart of the bred theory is the belief that leadership can be defined by a set of "success behaviors" that can be developed with preparation and practice. Furthermore, behaviors that produce "leadership failure" can also be defined, adding another layer to leadership training: what *not* to do. This "learn today, lead tomorrow" model remains the theory of choice for most leadership experts today.

TRUTH OR CONSEQUENCES

As a psychologist concerned with how these theories impact parenting, I think both models contain an element of truth. Leadership guru John Maxwell gave me this response when I asked him if leaders were "born or bred": "They're born," he said. "I've yet to meet one that came into the world any other way!" Very funny. He went on to state that while some people are born with certain natural leadership gifts, the ability to lead is a collection of skills that can be acquired and advanced.[5]

This is an encouragement to both parents and kids. While *competence* accounts for the skills of a leader and *character* accounts for the fiber of a leader, neither are innate. Both can be developed. Even if our sons and daughters were followers as four-year-olds, that doesn't mean they're destined to be dominated by the Sampsons of the world for the rest of their lives. At least, not if we have anything to say about it!

THE TRUTH

Some people have natural leadership gifts . . . but almost anyone can learn how to lead.

As parents it's important for us to understand that leaders are learners. "Born" leaders tend to learn from experience; "bred" leaders tend to learn from the textbook. Both are better off if their parents step up to the leadership podium and challenge them with a few leadership lessons.

Eight Lessons in Leadership

Here are my suggestions for lessons every future leader ought to learn:

1. *The Significance of Self-Confidence.* The first person you'll ever lead will be yourself. If you wouldn't follow you, then why would anyone else? Be the kind of person that you would want to follow, and over time others will come to the same conclusion.

2. *The Significance of One.* In order to convince the people of Philadelphia of the advantages of street lighting, Benjamin Franklin decided to show his neighbors how compelling a single light could be. He bought a lantern, polished the glass, and placed it on a long bracket extending from his home. As darkness descended, he ignited the wick, and his neighbors soon noticed the warm glow in front of his residence. Most noticed that the light from this lantern helped them avoid tripping over the raised stones in the roadway. Before long, many of his neighbors placed lanterns in front of their own homes, and eventually the entire city recognized the need for well-lit streets. Philadelphia became the first city with street lights in America.[6]

   Still doubt the significance that one person can make?

3. *The Significance of Joining, Not Judging.* In the early 1980s, Chicago experienced a rash of gang-related slayings in a large inner-city housing project. Law enforcement agencies were unable to bring an end to the violence. For several weeks Mayor Jane Byrne challenged the police

and the people of Chicago to solve the problem. Finally, to everyone's surprise, the mayor announced that she was moving into the area herself. The city was shocked, but the local community supported the mayor's action. They decided that if the mayor of Chicago was willing to live with them and lead from within, then they were going to join her efforts.

Change didn't take long. Within months the crime rate dropped, respect was restored, and hope returned to an area where it had been lost.[7] That's the power of joining!

4. *The Significance of a Cause.* In the mid 1800s, Italian leader Guiseppe Garibaldi recruited men to fight the invaders of his country. He was looking for patriots. When asked what the reward would be for those who fought with him, he replied, "I give you neither pay nor quarters nor provisions. I offer hunger, thirst, battle, and death." Then he added, "Let him who loves this country with his whole heart, not just with his lips, follow me."

Garibaldi's forces were constantly undermanned and underequipped. But his famous quote, "Rome or death!" inspired his volunteers to push forward. Despite many setbacks, Garibaldi ended up unifying his country and became known as Italy's Sword of Unification. He was a leader because he believed in a cause; he was successful because he got others to believe also.[8]

5. *The Significance of Simplicity.* Vince Lombardi, the legendary coach of the Green Bay Packers, produced one NFL championship team after another. He motivated his men to play every moment of every game to the

best of their ability. No matter what the circumstances, the Packers were as strong and tough in the last two minutes as they were at the opening kickoff. What was his secret? Lombardi began each practice by holding up a football and saying, "Men, this is a football!" Then he drilled his players on the basics of blocking, tackling, and playmaking. As a leader, Lombardi proved that simple people make the complex hard—smart people make the complex simple.[9]

6. *The Significance of Action.* During his famous valley campaign, Civil War general Stonewall Jackson needed to get his army to the other side of the river. He ordered his engineers to build a bridge for the troops to cross. Later that afternoon he emphasized again the importance of crossing the river as soon as possible. Noticing that the engineers remained in their tent planning the bridge, a wagon master set to work. Soon he had the soldiers gathering up all the fence rails, logs, and rocks they could find. Within hours the crude bridge was finished and the wagon master was able to report to the general that all the wagons and artillery were on the other side of the river. When General Jackson asked, "Where are the engineers who were responsible for building the bridge?" the wagon master replied, "Still in their tent drawing up plans."[10]

It's good to make plans. It's even better to act on them!

7. *The Significance of Pulling, Not Pushing.* President Dwight D. Eisenhower demonstrated the art of leadership in a

simple but forceful way. He placed a single piece of string on a table and said to his Cabinet, "Pull it, and it follows wherever you want it to go. Push it, and it goes nowhere."[11] His point? Those who rely on leadership stand out in front and pull; those who rely on power stand in the back and push. Leadership trumps power any day.

8. *The Significance of Sacrifice.* Many have heard of the great Colosseum in Rome and the life-and-death fights of the ancient gladiators, but few are aware of the greatest Roman warrior of all. In AD 400, Telemachus, a monk from the countryside, traveled to the great city of Rome, believing it to be the center of Christianity. While in Rome, Telemachus happened upon the Colosseum and attended the games. That day the games were particularly violent, as gladiators fought to their death while the crowds cheered.

Telemachus was so appalled by this display of barbarism that he jumped into the arena, stood between two of the gladiators, and pleaded with them to stop the bloodshed. The crowd howled its displeasure, and the two gladiators pushed Telemachus to the side. Undeterred, the monk once again placed himself between the warriors. Now the audience was incensed and began calling for the holy man's blood.

One of the gladiators drew his sword and slew Telemachus on the spot. Suddenly the arena grew quiet. The slaying of an innocent man had filled the people's consciences with shame. History records that this was the last life that was ever taken in the Roman Colosseum.[12] One man, one purpose, one price tag. Period.

Being an Influence

Benjamin Franklin, Mayor Byrne, Lombardi, Garibaldi, the wagon master, Eisenhower, Telemachus—each of these individuals influenced the lives of those around them. Influence made a difference, and that's what made each of them a leader.

As parents we are leaders. We may not be a president in charge of thousands or a principal in charge of hundreds, but we do have influence in the lives of our children. And what can be more important than that? Our kids may determine their dreams, but our leadership will play a big part in determining their success.

Let's go back to Benjamin Bunny Preschool. Your child may be a follower today, but with training he could be a leader tomorrow. Who knows? He may even become Sampson's boss one day. What will make the difference? You. If you embrace and impart the belief that leaders are born, not bred, then your child is destined to follow that belief. It's the self-fulfilling prophecy. But if you believe that leadership can be learned, and you make every effort to encourage your child with lessons on leadership that will help him succeed, then he will have the tools he needs to lead.

Have doubts? A search of the Scriptures demonstrates that God shows up in unexpected places and calls unlikely leaders to do unbelievable tasks. Just look at the lives of Moses, Gideon, and Peter. Who but God could have seen their leadership potential?

If we teach our kids to *follow* these lessons on leadership, soon people will follow our kids. If we teach our kids to *live* these lessons in leadership, soon we will live in a different world, led by different people, heading in a different direction.

The leaders of tomorrow live right under our noses today. If we challenge them to *learn* today, they'll *lead* tomorrow. After all, leadership traits aren't just caught . . . they're also taught.

Kids don't have to be "born" leaders to lead.
Change this notion, and we'll change this nation.

THE LIE

Your Past Determines
Your Future

PREDICTION IS DIFFICULT,
ESPECIALLY WHEN IT COMES TO THE FUTURE.

Niels Bohr

Amanda is a seventeen-year-old high-school student living with her parents in Roanoke, Virginia. Recently her parents purchased a 2001 powder blue, two-door Honda Civic for her to drive to school and work. Her annual insurance premium is $978.

Mike is a seventeen-year-old high-school student living with his parents in Chicago, Illinois. Recently his parents purchased a 2001 dark blue, two-door Honda Civic for him to drive to school and work. His annual insurance premium is $2,115.

The difference is $1,137 per year.

Renee is a forty-one-year-old secretary living in Salt Lake City, Utah. She doesn't smoke and has no history of hypertension, elevated cholesterol, or other health problems. When applying for a $100,000, five-year, renewable, term life insurance policy, she was told her annual premium would be $321.

Eric is a forty-one-year-old ironworker living in Philadelphia, Pennsylvania. He doesn't smoke and has no history of hypertension, elevated cholesterol, or other health problems. When applying for a $100,000, five-year, renewable, term life insurance policy, he was told his annual premium would by $541.

The difference is $220 per year.

The Stanley family owns a three-bedroom, two-and-a-half-bath home on Bent Trail Drive in Cleveland, Ohio. Their two-story home was built in 1993 and is 3,310 square feet. They have fire detectors in every room, as well as a home-security system. Their annual homeowners insurance premium is $923.

The Slocum family owns a three-bedroom, two-and-a-half-bath home on Bent Creek Drive in Wichita, Texas. Their two-story home was built in 1993 and is 3,125 square feet. They installed fire detectors in every room, as well as a home-security system. Their annual homeowners insurance premium is $1,682.

The difference is $759 per year.

These lopsided premiums must be the result of unethical, double-dealing con artists practicing flagrant discrimination, brazen prejudice, or outrageous chauvinism—right? What else would account for these discrepancies? Actually, a review of the premiums found them to be fair, just, and legal. So says the American Academy of Actuaries.

Actuaries aren't charlatans reading tea leaves; they're well-trained professionals with college degrees who've studied such things as data analysis, statistical analysis, linear regression, and forecast confidence intervals. Considered one of the top five jobs in America,[1] actuaries are paid—and paid well—to analyze the past and predict the future. In 2003, associate actuaries earned an average of $99,500.[2]

On the street they're known as "number crunchers." On the job they're known as "risk calculators." They spend their time developing probability tables that estimate the likelihood of disasters, death, and disability. How exciting! I say that if actuaries are smart enough to know I'm probably going to have an accident on the way to work this month, why not call me, and I'll stay home? Is it too much to ask a life-insurance actuary to take a few minutes out of his or her day to inform me that I'm expected to die this year? Now, that would be customer service!

Actuaries predict the future based on the past. In the examples cited above, they determined that:

- As a male teenager living in a large city, Mike is three times more likely than Amanda to have a car accident this year. That's why his insurance premium cost $1,137 more than Amanda's.

- As a forty-one-year-old male working in a high risk profession, Eric is four times less likely than Renee to see his sixtieth birthday. That's why his insurance premium cost $220 more than Renee's.

- The Slocum home is smack dab in the middle of "Tornado Alley" and is six times more likely to suffer tornado damage than the Stanley home in Ohio. That's why their insurance premium cost $759 more than the Stanleys'.

Enter the data. Apply the equation. Forecast the future. Actuaries do it, companies rely on it, management counts on it, and shareholders depend on it. But just because a scalpel works for a cardiologist doesn't mean it will work for a carpenter. The principles of probability may work for actuaries predicting disasters—but not for parents predicting the fate of their children. Those foolish enough to apply probabilities to raising kids are like the travelers who drowned while crossing a river described by the natives as having an "average depth" of four feet. "Average" leaves a lot of room for exceptions.

Painful Past, Promising Future

If the past determines the future, then Cheryl Green didn't have a chance. I met Cheryl five years ago. She was not a child of privilege, prestige, or position. As a matter of fact, her childhood would best be described as a life of pain rather than plenty.

Cheryl authored a book called *Child of Promise: One Woman's Journey from Tragedy to Triumph.*[3] The first ten words of the book read, "I thank you, God, for my life, including my past." Frankly, her past isn't anything I'd give thanks for. It involved disability, racism, sexual abuse, poverty, homelessness, mental illness, and a mother who tried to murder her.

Cheryl is an African-American woman who grew up in Houston in a wooden shack, the daughter of sharecroppers who worked for wealthy whites in the oppressive Texas heat. Born in 1970, she was a sight to behold. When the doctor first placed the blanket-bound newborn in her mother's arms, Cheryl's mom ran her fingers through the tiny girl's hair, kissed each one of her ten fragile fingers, unwrapped the blanket . . . and fainted. Faultless from the waist up, Cheryl was flawed from the waist down. Something had gone wrong. Her legs were curved in a bow, her ankles were missing, her toes were misplaced. No philanthropic foundations, no medical miracles, and no Jerry Lewis telethons existed for people like Cheryl.

But Cheryl was about to discover that there are far worse problems than having a physical disability.

Despite the challenges of having a disabled child, Cheryl's parents inched forward. Dad became a chemist; Mom, a dietician. For a while they experienced the good life: a home, two cars, family vacations. Then tragedy struck. It was as swift as it was sweeping. First, one of Cheryl's grandmothers died; then her dad's best friend passed away. Cheryl's mom suffered a blood clot in her lung and tumors in her uterus. In the process, jobs were lost, dreams were lost, hope was lost. Possessions dwindled while problems doubled. Her parents' marital malfunction was anesthetized by an affair.

By any measure, the family was in freefall, spiraling down the socioeconomic ladder from helplessness to hopelessness to homelessness. Eventually their home was a four-door sedan. Cheryl's playground was the back seat. When they became frustrated with sleeping in the car, the family spent their nights in a rented storage facility with no electricity, no water, and no air conditioning.

They would never return to a life of stability again. Mental illness seized control of both parents. Fear held them captive, while paranoia kept them paralyzed. Fingers were pointed and tempers flared. Verbal abuse was common; sexual abuse was coming. To her parents, Cheryl became a "poster child"—at least when they were applying for food stamps. To her well-intentioned doctors, she became the subject of medical research, a cross between a medical celebrity and a medical aberration.

There would be no cure for Cheryl, which only served to amplify her mom's depression and accelerate her dad's drinking.

Unable to cope with demanding problems and diminishing resources, her parents decided to leave Cheryl and her older sister in the hands of her grandmother. The first words Cheryl remembers hearing from her grandmother's lips were, "This is one ugly child." Grandma then asked Cheryl's uncle—a drug addict, an ex-con, and a schizophrenic—to figure out what to do with the girl. When he tried to "cleanse" Cheryl with the blood of a dead chicken, seven-year-old Cheryl and her nine-year-old sister hobbled eight miles to their aunt's home . . . where later that summer Cheryl was molested by her cousin.

What could be worse than being molested? How about being murdered? At one point when Cheryl's mother was struggling with schizophrenic delusions, she attempted to take Cheryl's life with a kitchen knife. Later, what her mother failed to accomplish, Cheryl considered completing after receiving a D in a class at school. In Cheryl's mind, academic failure meant there was little chance of success in her future and even less hope for her heart in the present. With a battered body, a broken home, a bruised heart, and a blemished report card, Cheryl believed that her future would be as painful as her past. The adults in her life had given her no reason to believe otherwise. Suicide seemed like the only solution.

Had it not been for the twin towers of promise that Cheryl held on to, she was destined for disaster. Together these towers were like crutches to the crippled. One provided strength for her struggles; the other provided hope for her future.

Her strength came from her schoolwork, and her hope came from her faith. School offered Cheryl a shelter from the thunderstorms of life—and this harbor had lights, air conditioning, and running water. Faith encouraged Cheryl to look up, not out, and not in. Cheryl found a personal relationship with God through Jesus Christ. That relationship offered her unbelievable peace, unconditional love, and unthinkable hope. School provided the flight path and faith provided the fuel that enabled her to escape from her dysfunctional past.

Upon graduation from high school, Cheryl was awarded a four-year scholarship to study psychology at Yale University. While there, she was awarded the David Everett Chantler Prize for "character, courage, and high moral purpose" for her work helping the U.S. Department of Justice implement the Americans with Disabilities Act of 1990. Following graduation from Yale, she attended Ohio State University for her master's degree and then Southern Methodist University for her PhD. For her academic success, Cheryl was recognized by the Mellon Foundation, the National Science Foundation, and the National Institute of Mental Health. She began her career in philanthropy with the Dole Foundation (created by former senator Bob Dole), managing a funding pool of $1.7 million to promote employment for the disabled. Today Dr. Cheryl Green is a college professor with her name on the door and her diplomas on the wall.

Cheryl's accomplishments seem unbelievable because her childhood was so unthinkable. Her parents, her grandmother, and the other adults in her family gave up on her. But despite her circumstances, Cheryl refused to believe she was bound by the past. She made wise choices about her future because she had her God and she had her goals. Frankly, you have to wonder if her decision to study psychology was intended to help others—or help herself. Ultimately she did both.

TRUTH OR CONSEQUENCES

Determinism is the term for what drives many to believe that the past dictates the future. Birthed by Socrates, promoted by Newton, and popularized by Pierre-Simon Laplace, determinism has had its foothold in our culture since the early nineteenth century. Simply put, determinism says that your current life is the product of your past and, more important, the determining factor for your future. You're bound by your genes, and you're a victim of your circumstances. You have no choice, no chance, and no control. There is no way out and no way up.

Recently defense attorneys have become the biggest defenders of determinism, arguing that their clients are helpless victims whose criminal behavior has been caused by bad genes, bad parents, bad schools, bad music, bad television, bad drugs, or bad potty training. Thankfully, most juries have said, "Nice try. Guilty as charged!"

But while juries may not buy determinism as a defense, many kids see it as a fact of their fate. They believe their future has little promise and their dreams have little potential. Why? Because that's what their parents have taught them. Unwittingly, parents promote this belief every time they voice messages such as:

- "You're just like your father"—it's genetic.

- "Fat as a child, fat as an adult"—it's hopeless.

- "Fail in school and you'll fail in life"—it's certain.

- "Once a thief, always a thief"—it's inevitable.

- "If it's meant to be, it will be. If not, then it wasn't meant to be"—it's predestined.

As parents we need to dispel this deception before it disables our kids. Cheryl Green and countless individuals like her prove that the past doesn't determine a person's future—vision does. Here's the truth our kids need to know:

THE TRUTH

Your past may *affect* the present,
but your vision—and your choices—
will determine your future.

There are three challenges to determinism that combat this fallacy faster than Clairol on gray hair. They are choice, chance, and the Creator. We need to teach these three Cs to our kids:

1. *Choice.* When I was growing up, I had four options at the ice-cream store: vanilla, chocolate, strawberry . . . or nothing. Since then, things have changed.

   Choice was invented by Baskin-Robbins. Enter any one of their 2,616 stores across America and your doctrine on determinism melts like ice cream under a heat lamp. You find yourself at the epicenter of choice: three different cones, three different scoop sizes, thirty-one different flavors. Staring into the freezer case, you're motionless, eyes glazed, mouth salivating. You're in the major leagues now. Only the brave can handle the pressure.

   There are few things in life you can count on, but this is one of them: different people prefer different desserts. When my family enters our local Baskin-Robbins store, you can count on me to order mint chocolate chip; my wife, Jenni, will have cookies 'n cream; eighteen-year-old Brittany will ask for rocky road; fourteen-year-old Cody will order chocolate-chip cookie dough; and our youngest, thirteen-year-old Courtney—well, she'll pick the one with the most colors in it! Here's the point: when our kids were young (and we were broke), we bought a half gallon of ice cream from the grocery store . . . and it was usually vanilla. Now we go to Baskin-Robbins. It's a whole new world.

> Choice equals options.
> Options equal change.
> Change equals opportunity.

Choice breaks the cycle that suggests your yesterdays will determine your tomorrow . . . and it does it *today*.

2. *Chance.* In 1947 former restaurant worker Jack Wurm found himself both penniless and jobless. One day as he was walking along a San Francisco beach, he came across an empty bottle filled only with a piece of paper. He pulled out the paper, read the note, and discovered that he had in his hands the last will and testament of Daisy Singer Alexander, heir to the Singer sewing-machine fortune. The note read: "To avoid confusion, I leave my entire estate to the lucky person who finds this bottle and to my attorney, Barry Cohen, share and share alike."[4]

Unbelievable as it may seem, the courts accepted that the heiress had written the note twelve years earlier and had thrown the bottle into the River Thames in London. Oceanographers believe the bottle made its way down the Thames, across the North Sea, above Scandinavia, Russia, and Siberia, through the Bering Straits, and into the Pacific Ocean, where it drifted south until it finally washed up on that San Francisco beach. Jack Wurm's discovery netted him more than $6 million in cash and Singer stock. One day he was an unemployed restaurant worker—the next day he could have bought the place.

Chance happens! Some call it coincidence, but for Christians it's more like "God-incidence"—God working in our lives in ways that we can't always predict. Whatever you call it, chance breaks the back of determinism in an instant.

Life is full of the unpredictable, the unexplainable, and the unforeseeable.

> A single "chance" encounter can
> change your future forever.

3. *The Creator.* While it may sound ridiculous to some people, prayer is the process by which you look heaven-ward and ask an invisible God to suspend the laws of the universe on your behalf. You ask an unseen God to meet an undeniable need—even if it takes a miracle. Crazy as it sounds, it works!

Actually, it turns out that most people don't think the idea of prayer is crazy. According to a recent *Newsweek* poll, 92 percent of all Americans believe in God, 84 percent believe in miracles, and 48 percent have personally experienced a miracle in their lives.[5]

As I find myself putting pen to paper to finish this chapter, I also find myself putting prayer to the test in another chapter—a chapter in life. Our family of five is about to become a family of four. By the time you read this, our eighteen-year-old daughter, Brittany, will have cleared her closet, stuffed her suitcases, and loaded her laptop into her Mustang in order to fly from this nest to the next. It's time for college. A new chapter in Brit's life means the end of a chapter in ours.

Brit's birth changed life for Jenni and me. Her arrival turned a woman into a mom, a man into a father, and a couple into a family. Over the years I've read Brit a thousand books, given Brit a thousand kisses, and whispered to God a thousand prayers—each with her name in it.

I believe in the power of prayer. Over the past few years I've prayed regularly about the wit and wisdom that would end up on the pages of this book. But over the past few decades I've prayed more often about the breadth of Brit's character and the depth of her convictions. The thought of her departure drives me to my knees. Not with agony, but with anticipation. Will she find the right roommate? Will she choose the right major? Will she commit to memory the right information? Will she fall romantically for the right guy? Will she brush and floss her teeth twice a day?

The prayers of the past have molded a girl into a woman. The prayers I whisper today will take her the rest of the way:

Yesterday I asked God to give Brit the desire to keep her room clean; today I ask God to give her the desire to keep her actions clean.

Yesterday I asked God to help Brit share her toys; today I ask God to help her share her faith.

Yesterday I asked God to take away the dreams that kept Brit awake at night; today I ask God to give her the dreams that will get her out of bed each morning.

Yesterday I asked God to give Brit the right friends to play with; today I ask God to give her the right guy to spend the rest of her life with.

Yesterday I asked God to protect Brit and keep her safe; today I ask God to stretch her and make her strong.

Yesterday I asked God to give Brit confidence that she might lead others; today I ask God to give her compassion that she might serve others.

I believe that prayer changes things, because I believe in a God who hears the prayers of a parent—and who is not bound by the past to determine a child's future. Just ask Cheryl Green. If it weren't for God, Cheryl would be another story in the newspaper or another statistic on a police log. But Cheryl's future was not determined by her past; it was determined by her beliefs, her vision, and her choices. She believed that her future was hers to determine, and that a God in heaven and an education here on earth would change her destiny. Any doctor worth his or her diploma will tell you this important truth: beliefs determine behaviors. Change a child's beliefs, and you'll change a child's behaviors. Change a child's behaviors, and you'll change a child's future.

Many in Brittany's world will tell her that her future is determined by her past. That's a lie. I tell her that faith in Christ allows her mistakes to be forgotten and her sins to be forgiven. I tell her that defeat exists only in her mind and that she has the power to let her memories limit her or launch her. Now let me ask you—what will you tell *your* kids?

Prayer changes things because God changes things.
Parents change a child's destiny the most
when they spend time on their knees.

10

THE LIE
You Can Have It All

... YOU JUST CAN'T HAVE IT ALL AT ONCE.

Oprah

I n the next few minutes I'm going to save you $3,875.

More on that later.

From an early age, Dana's kids were told they could have it all. They were provided private schools for their education, role models for their inspiration, and twenty-dollar bills for their motivation. They were told they could win any game, conquer any challenge, overcome any obstacle. They were destined for the Promised Land—a city called Success. Welcome to America!

By anyone's standards, fourteen-year-old Amanda, fifteen-year-old Nathan, and eighteen-year-old Dillon *were* successful. Each stood at the top of his or her class academically, as well as athletically. Weekdays were filled with schoolwork, homework, and busywork. Filling in the gaps were cheerleading, basketball, and tennis. God got seventy minutes at church on Sunday mornings.

Dana challenged her kids to conquer substandard and

second-rate performance with discipline and determination. She encouraged them to prevail over a giant called "mediocrity" that lumbered across the landscape of other people's lives. She wanted more for her kids. She wanted more for herself. She believed she deserved more. This was her one shot, and she intended to "grab for the gusto." Unfortunately, Dana's desire became her children's demon. Mom set the standard higher than the kids could hurdle. Failing and frustrated, the kids felt that enough was never enough . . . and more was not an option.

This castle was about to crumble.

Living beyond Mediocrity

Dana wanted it all. Who doesn't?

Who gets up in the morning and says, "Today I want to be a mediocre person and live a mediocre life. I want a mediocre marriage with a mediocre spouse. I want to raise mediocre kids and send them to mediocre schools that will teach them to become mediocre surgeons, mediocre scientists, and mediocre schoolteachers. Today I'm happy to live in my mediocre home and drive a mediocre car. I'm glad to go to my mediocre job, where I'm surrounded by mediocre coworkers and paid a mediocre paycheck that doesn't even cover the payments on my mediocre Sears credit card."

Dana certainly didn't. She wanted to live a life that was great tasting . . . *and* less filling. She was hungry and wanted to order the whole menu, not just a meal. She believed she was entitled to the "whole enchilada"—not just two tacos, a bean salad, and a Diet Coke. Dana wasn't content to "keep up with the Joneses." She wanted to see them in her rear-view mirror. She didn't just want to drive in the fast lane; she wanted to live there.

Dana was what *Newsweek* called in an eleven-page special report "a success seeker" whose work was personally meaningful, emotionally satisfying, and selected for self-expression.[1] As a forty-seven-year-old, upwardly mobile Yuppie, she was determined to have it all—and expecting someone else to pick up the tab.

According to *Newsweek*, she's not alone.

I met Dana a few years ago while in private practice. She was a single parent who described herself as a "full-time mom, full-time Realtor, and full-time chauffeur." (Does anyone see a problem here?) As a child, Dana learned about the 3 Rs. As an adult she redefined them: rich, relational, and ravishing.

From our first meeting, Dana appeared to be extremely accomplished and exceptionally proficient. Professionally, she was on the fast track in the real-estate business. Personally, she was banking on her two-year MBA and her six-figure divorce settlement to pave the way for her to have it all, do it all . . . *be* it all.

Unfortunately, she ran into a few bumps in the road.

> The stress of success was killing her.
> It wasn't doing much for her kids either.

Dana's kids didn't know it, but Mom's two best friends were Maalox and Alka-Seltzer. She never left home without them. She was a reluctant patient, referred to my office by her physician after three trials of antianxiety and antidepressant medications resulted in little improvement. The doctor had no tricks left in his medical bag. No pill was strong enough to fix this modern-day malady.

Dana grew up feeling like a secondhand child in a

secondhand family settling for a secondhand life. Her clothes were her sister's hand-me-downs, and her boyfriends in high school fit the same description. During college everything changed: she met Rich, who was just what his name implied. He wore the finest clothes, drove the finest car, and had the finest family credentials. Saved from her slavery of mediocrity, Dana grew accustomed to her new lifestyle with Rich. They married; they went to graduate school; they had children.

For the next decade, Dana was on the fast track to "having it all." Along the way she pushed to make sure her kids would "have it all" too. What's good for the goose is good for the gander, she figured. She wanted her kids to move from mediocre to manicured, just as she had.

The divorce was a speed bump Dana hadn't expected. At that point she saw two options from which she could choose. Plan A would take her backward to her mediocre, secondhand life. Plan B would take her forward to a land of plenty and a state of abundance. Dana determined there was no looking back. She could still have it all—and have it now. What's more, she could teach her kids that the brass ring is there for those who choose to grab it.

Fast-forward three years, three boyfriends, and three pre-scriptions later. Dillon was on his way home from college—permanently. The school had had enough of his C-minus grades and D-minus behavior. Nathan was skipping classes in his senior year in high school, and Amanda was skipping homes—to live with her dad. Despite her size 2 business suits and Kate Spade handbags, Dana's life and her family were un-raveling before her eyes. Weak and wanting, Dana was ready to explore Plan C.

TRUTH OR CONSEQUENCES

Our dreams create it. Our culture promotes it. Our nature says we deserve it. So when our kids ask, we say, "Sure, honey. You can have it all!"

That's what Dana believed. She thought she was entitled to:

- Spend without saving

- Eat without expanding

- Mature without aging

- Vacation without spending

- Have her cake and eat it too!

And why not? We live in a land of abundance. Advertisers tell us we're just one purchase away from "paradise." Whether it's a new couch, a new computer, or a new car, the people in the commercials can hardly contain themselves as they contemplate the joy of making their new purchase. (Of course, we never see them when the Visa bill arrives).

Beer companies promise great taste that's less filling. Gas fireplaces offer flames without the fuss. Investment brokers offer rewards without risk, women's seminars promote babies *and* boardrooms, and articles in *Allure* promise incredible sex . . . while doing the dishes!

And therein is the lie: That life can be a payoff without a price tag, pleasure without a payment. That a person can "have it all" without "giving it all" to achieve it.

THE TRUTH

*Everything of value costs something.
You* can't *have it all, but you* can *have
a lot . . . as long as you're
willing to pay the price for it.*

As parents we must teach our kids that everything of value costs something. *Everything.* It may cost money, it may cost time, it may even cost our health; but everything has a cost. Telling our kids that they can "have it all" and implying that there isn't a price to pay promotes poor decision making on their part . . . and a lack of credibility on ours.

Our goal must be to teach our kids how to make healthy decisions. They do that by trading lower-order priorities for higher-order priorities, not by thinking they can get what they want for free. Kids who are healthy decision makers have learned how to trade something they have for something they want—and they've learned to pay the difference.

Every decision has a cost. Every yes comes with a no. It's like up and down, day and night, good and bad, in and out; they go together. If we say yes to a cheeseburger, we're saying no to grilled chicken. If we say yes to french fries, we're saying no to a side salad. If we say yes to a soda, we're saying no to iced tea. And if we say yes to all three with any regularity, we're saying no to ever meeting our grandkids!

Why do parents miss the mark? We want our kids to have what we lacked growing up. We remember being left out, left alone, or left behind. We want a different life for our children— and we're willing to finance it. Most of us would gladly work a little harder, run a little longer, or jump a little higher if we thought it would bring a handful of happiness to our kids. We're more than willing to sacrifice our needs to meet theirs, to deny our wants to provide for theirs. Unfortunately, we rob them of the growth we gained and the lessons we learned when we hand them life on a silver platter. For most of us it was when tears filled our eyes and pain filled our hearts that we learned the value of a dollar, the value of a friend, and the value of a hug.

The truth is, while we'd like to believe that "having it all" ensures "happiness for all," it doesn't—not for us, and not for our children. Consider the success and celebrity status that came to the kids in the legendary 1930s movie series *Our Gang*, which ran as movie shorts in the late 1930s. (Later, in the 1950s, it became a syndicated TV show renamed *The Little Rascals*.) You would think that starring in this hit series would have delivered abundant riches and ample rewards to its young cast. Unfortunately, most experienced ruin and ravage instead:

- "Alfalfa" (Carl Switzer) was shot to death at age thirty-one.

- "Chubby" (Norman Chaney) died following surgery at age eighteen.

- "Buckwheat" (William Thomas) died from a heart attack at forty-nine.

- "Froggy" (William Laughline) was killed in a motor scooter accident at sixteen.

- "Brisbane" (Kendall McComas) committed suicide at age sixty-four.

- "Stymie" (Mathew Bear) lived a life of drug abuse, served jail time, and died at age fifty-six.

- "Wheezer" (Robert Hutchins) was killed in an airplane accident at nineteen.

- "Darla" (Darla Hood, the *Our Gang* leading lady) died of hepatitis at forty-seven.

- "Bonedust" (Robert H. Young) died in a hotel fire at thirty-four.

- "Dorothy" (Dorothy Dandridge) committed suicide at forty-two.

- "Deadpan" (Harold Switzer) was murdered at forty-two.

- "Pete the Pup" was thought to be poisoned by food laced with glass.[2]

Countering the Lie

What can you as a parent do to counter the "you can have it all" mentality that permeates so much of our culture? Let me suggest the following:

1. *Encourage your kids to pursue success in three simple areas: passion, purpose, and hope.* This can be accomplished by helping them find:

   - Someone significant to love

   - Something significant to do

   - Something significant to look forward to

   If your kids live lives that are centered on the pursuit of these goals, then despite what others may think, they are well on the way to "having it all." Just ask those who've lived long enough to know.

2. *In a culture driven by abundance, choose the road of "contentment." Then model it for your kids to see.* "More" has become the caffeine of our culture. Enough is never enough. When we can't afford "more," we finance it. As a result the average American household has accrued more than $18,000 in nonmortgage consumer debt.[3] Kids see their parents handcuffed by debt and plagued by their payments. Many have concluded that "battling over the budget" is as normal as milk with cereal.

Solomon was known for his wealth and his wisdom. Born about one thousand years before Christ, he became king of Israel in 971 BC. Solomon denied himself no worldly pleasure or human possession. He's one guy who "had it all." He wrote:

> I made my works great, I built myself houses and planted myself vineyards. I made myself gardens and orchards, and I planted all kinds of fruit trees in them. . . . Yes, I had greater possessions of herds and flocks than all who were in Jerusalem before me. I also gathered for myself silver and gold and the special treasures of kings and of the provinces. . . . So I became great and excelled more than all who were before me in Jerusalem. (Ecclesiastes 2:4–9 NKJV)

Yet Solomon concluded, "Then I looked at all the work my hands had done and on the labor in which I had toiled; and indeed all was vanity and grasping for the wind" (v. 11).

Solomon had it all—except for the one thing he longed for: contentment. This one attribute has made many a poor man rich, and its lack has made many a rich man poor. The grass may be greener on the other side of the fence, but it still has to be mowed!

3. *Encourage your kids to appreciate what they have while they have it.* A man named Mike from Miami Lakes, Florida, offered an unusual response when he was asked, "Do you have it all?" He stated that he would have—if he could have "just five more minutes." Why five more minutes? Well, Catherine, his wife of fifteen months, had just passed away, and Mike would have traded everything he had for just five more minutes:

- Minute 1: to tell Catherine how much he appreciated her

- Minute 2: to tell her how much he believed in her

- Minute 3: to tell her how much he respected her

- Minute 4: to hold her and tell her how much he loved her

- Minute 5: to say goodbye and wish her peace and comfort forever[4]

What about you? If you knew that everything you have would be gone tomorrow, how would you live your life today? What would you say to your spouse, your kids, your coworkers? You never know when "late" is "too late." Teach your kids to appreciate what they have by watching you acknowledge what you value.

4. *Let your kids know you believe in them.* Most kids respond well when challenged to "raise the bar," as long as they

sense that we believe they can leap to a new level. Our prayer is that they'll succeed. Our belief is that by raising the bar, they'll try a little harder and maximize their effort. When kids know that their parents, coaches, and teachers believe in them, the effect is contagious and they begin to believe in themselves. It's a self-fulfilling prophecy—and that's a good thing.

But here's a tip: make sure you communicate motivation, not expectation. Underachievement is rooted in the fear of failure; therefore, telling your kids that you think they can "bring home the gold" or "have it all" creates stress, not support—an unrealistic expectation, not a healthy motivation.

If your children are "underachievers," redefine success as progress, not perfection. For some kids, success may be trying out for a team (not just making it), getting straight Cs (instead of Ds), or eating healthy foods (rather than harmful ones). Then pour on the praise, and let success pave the way for progress. With kids nothing motivates more than success, and nothing frustrates more than failure. Tell your children how proud you are of them, morning, noon, and night. Remember, behavior that's rewarded is behavior that's repeated.

5. *Teach your kids the concept of "cost."* This will improve their decision-making abilities greatly. With your encouragement your kids will be able to achieve great things in their lives; but everything they gain *will* have a price tag. Teach them to set priorities and make wise choices. There are no free lunches in this world. Beware of those who offer one!

Speaking of choices, remember Dana? She's the single mom who believed the lie, thinking that she could "have it all" with few (if any) costs to pay. Well, faced with significant personal and parental challenges, she discovered that her affluent lifestyle and ambitious career goals were costing her what she valued most: her health and her family. So she made some wise choices. She downsized her home and right sized her priorities. She also took the pressure off her kids to "have it all," "do it all," and "be it all"—and her kids responded. Dillon eventually returned to college, Nathan stopped skipping classes, and Amanda returned home. The last time I heard from Dana, she said, "After more than a year of therapy, I learned that you *can* have it all. You just can't have it *all at once.*"

That insight cost Dana $3,875 in therapy bills.

You got it for the price of this book.

THE LIE

It's Not What You Know but Who You Know That Counts

A GOOD LAWYER KNOWS THE LAW.
A GREAT LAWYER KNOWS THE JUDGE.

Lance was just like most kids—first he saw it, then he simulated it.

Growing up on the tumbleweed terrain of West Texas had its share of challenges, but it also had its benefits. Located halfway between Fort Worth and El Paso, Midland was always considered a small town. It was absent of big-city crime, big-city prices, and big-city egos. People were friendly. They knew their neighbors and went out of their way to be cheerful, helpful, and thankful.

Lance's father, Ted, was the third generation of his family to call Midland home. Family roots ran deep—and so did relationships. Ted knew everyone in town, from the dog catcher to the watch maker. Midland was just that kind of place.

Academically, Ted never made it past high school. Truth be told, he never returned to complete the twelfth grade. Times were different back then—especially in Midland. The town discovered oil. Lots of it.

Ted got a job working on an oil rig when he was just seventeen. Ted's uncle hired the crew, managed the crew, and fired the crew. No unions. No lawyers. No EEOC. That's just the way it was back then in Midland.

Over the course of his career, Ted was promoted to crew chief, field supervisor, and finally, operations manager. Honestly (Ted would be the first to admit it) his promotions had less to do with his oil IQ and supervisory skills and more to do with the fact that his childhood sidekick was the company vice president. His buddy wanted Ted at his side, just like the good old days.

When Ted was caught speeding, warnings were given rather than tickets. Ted knew most of the officers on the force. When Ted needed a loan—no problem, the banker was his buddy. When Ted needed a vehicle—you guessed it, a friend of the family found just the right car . . . cheap.

Then things got interesting. In 1982 Ted was accused of tax evasion. The case was heard, and a verdict was handed down: not guilty. Insiders say the verdict was based more on being tried before a "jury of his peers" than the evidence.

Ted loved living in Midland. To him it was like living in the promised land.

Lance expected to experience the same hometown hospitality in Midland that his father did. When Lance quit school at age seventeen, he had his father's blessing. Ted told his son, "Don't worry, I've got enough friends in this town to take care of both of us."

Unfortunately, things didn't turn out as well for Lance
as they both expected.

Let's Make a Deal

Three hundred and thirteen miles east of Midland, Texas, is a place so close to heaven, it would turn an atheist's heart toward God. Even better, it's only fifteen minutes from my front door.

For those who think a golf course is just a golf course . . . you haven't been to Vaquero Golf Club. Metallic name plates hang over locker doors and include the names of several pro golfers who make their livings on the links (including Byron Nelson). According to assistant pro Greg Morris, service is Vaquero's moniker, and their response to your most lavish request is typically, "Yes, sir."

"Each member will have a profile—from shirt size to food preference—and when a member drives through the gate, we will know who the person is," Morris says. "He will be greeted, helped by valet parking, and if he wants us to take care of his dry cleaning or wash his car while he is playing golf, we will take care of it." When club members reach the practice tee, they find Titleist Pro V1 golf balls stacked in pyramids for their pleasure and a uniformed caddie (or cart) at their disposal.

As golfers leave the ninth green, they are greeted by an attendant with a "howdy" and a damp towel to clean their hands for what comes next. Beside the tenth tee box is a country-club treat: a gourmet chef with an array of appetizers designed to tantalize the taste buds. Then it's time for the main meal—anything from brats and beer to smoked duck. And just like eating at Sonic, you dine in your cart!

Besides having a caddy on call and a spread-for-every-sportsman, what possesses some of my neighbors to put up

Vaquero's $180,000 annual membership fee? They tell me, "This is where the deals are done."

It's not a fee. It's an investment.

Somewhere on the manicured fairways of this 7,064-yard golf course, proposals are presented, prices are negotiated, and deals are consummated with a handshake. Lawyers take care of the details later.

Making Connections

When I was a kid playing around my father's workshop, I thought "making connections" was soldering two pieces of wire together. When I was in college, I thought "making connections" was spending time in the lobby of the girls' dorm collecting phone numbers. When I became a neuropsychologist, I thought "making connections" was helping patients develop new neuronal pathways following a stroke or head injury. Today, the concept of "making connections" has taken on new meaning . . . and that's not necessarily a good thing.

Like most parents, the message I've preached to my kids as they've grown up has been: if you study hard and apply yourself in school, you will not only do well in the classroom, you will eventually end up in the boardroom. School is a critical laboratory that not only teaches the three Rs of academic development, but also the three Rs of professional development: relationships, responsibility, and resolve. As our kids hear these principles, value these principles, and apply these principles, they develop the minds of successful professionals.

Unfortunately, society preaches a different message. Our kids will conclude that academic achievement is highly overrated if they are led to believe that success is more a product of their golf membership than their grade point average. If the saying is true that "It's not what you know but who you know that counts," then forget studying! If connections grease the wheel of success, why not spend more time in the lunchroom and less time in the classroom?

That's a good question. Sociologists tell us that in some circles "social capital" is more valuable than a college degree or a purse full of cash. Simply put, connections open doors. Kids can't help but see it:

- Want to run for office? Better know the mayor.

- Want a promotion? Better know someone in the carpeted offices.

- Want to be in pictures? Better know a Hollywood producer.

- Want to attend law school? Better know a judge.

- Want a great deal on a used car? Better know a salesman.

- Want tickets to a Cowboys game? Sorry, you'll need connections . . .

Ironically, we live in the information age. That would suggest that the more you know, the further you'll go. Apparently that memo never got out. By all appearances, from Hollywood to Washington, the road to the good life is paved by the people you know, not what you know. Connections are the pathway to power, prestige, and popularity.

At least they were for Tori and George.

In Hollywood, five-foot-six Tori is a mover and shaker. When she was seventeen years old, she costarred with Luke

Perry, Shannen Doherty, and Jason Priestley in the 1990 hit TV series, *Beverly Hills 90210*. Since then she has gone on to appear in more than twenty movies and TV series. You may recognize her last name: Spelling. Tori is the daughter of Aaron Spelling, the man who produced nearly every TV show on the ABC network in the 1970s. I wonder if he had anything to do with his daughter's career success?[1]

At the other end of the country lies Washington, D.C., probably the most "connected" city in America. While there is some dispute regarding the role that his father played in his admission to the Texas Air National Guard, there is little doubt that our forty-third president, George W. Bush, was aided by his dad when it came to his academic pursuits. While George's high-school grades were weak, his family connections were strong—ensuring his admission to one of the most prestigious Ivy League schools in America: Yale University. And although it is widely known that George was a C student at Yale, after graduation he was admitted to the most prominent business school in America: Harvard.[2]

That's interesting—C must stand for "connected."

TRUTH OR CONSEQUENCES

Unfortunately, a message that communicates to our kids that success is based on who they know rather than what they know only serves to minimize their academic efforts. It also promotes the misconception that someone, somewhere, somehow will carry them to the promised land. Inherent in this motto is the implication that networking means "not working" and that social capital matters more than scholastic achievement.

Connections *can* be important. That's life. And while some people may be able to grease the wheels of success with social capital, I don't want to encourage my kids to count on "who they know" as their tickets to triumph at school or at work. As parents, we must do our best to dispel the lie that connections will be enough to carry our kids to the top of the totem pole. If we don't, we're encouraging laziness, promoting apathy, and potentially setting them up for a lifetime of disappointment and failure.

The fact is, who you know isn't enough to make you successful in life. For that matter, neither is what you know.

THE TRUTH

It's not about what you know . . . or who you know. It's what you do with what you know that matters most.

While grades are good, they're not enough. While creativity is good, it's not enough. While connections are good, they're not enough. Einstein wasn't successful because he had good grades, good ideas, or good connections. He was successful because of what he *did* with them. What you know doesn't matter unless you do something with it. Here are a few things to tell your kids about making the most of what and who they know.

1. *Hard work trumps intelligence, social status, and family background.* In a classic study, Harvard researchers Dr. George Vaillant and Caroline Vaillant found that success in adulthood is more related to hard work than to intelligence, social status, or family background. Their

study involved 465 individuals followed from adolescence to their midforties. They discovered that those who worked the hardest as children (household chores, part-time jobs, sports, and studies) were the highest-paid and most satisfied adults later in life. The least hardworking kids experienced greater unemployment, unhappiness, and earlier death.[3]

We once had a cat named Mocha. On most days Mocha sat perched atop the furniture looking for prey (more from curiosity than from craving). Cautious and calculating, Mocha would "measure twice, leap once." On most occasions success was her reward. Compare Mocha to our present cat—P-Kitty. On most days P-Kitty sits perched atop the furniture much like her predecessor. The difference between the two cats is that P-Kitty often looks . . . but seldom leaps.

Knowledge may be power,
but action turns power into accomplishment.

2. *Connections must be coupled with personal plans and actions.*
Remember Lance? Lance was seventeen and ready to master the town of Midland, just as his father did. Initially Lance found work in the oil fields, where the jobs were numerous and the pay generous. Dad made a few phone calls to make sure Lance was put on the fast track. "It's all about who you know," he told his son. So Lance settled into the "good life," fully expecting to enjoy the same privilege, prosperity, and pardon his father experienced. After all, he had connections.

Then the oil industry turned from boom to bust.

The year was 1986. In just a few years the price of oil plummeted from $31 a barrel to just $12. Independent oil companies filed for bankruptcy faster than you could spell o-i-l. The unemployment rate skyrocketed in Midland—leaving Lance with no job, no high-school diploma, and no backup plan. To make matters worse, his father passed away in the winter of 1987. Lance lost his father as well as his *connection to his connections.*

I'd like to tell you that Lance picked himself up, got his GED, went to college, and is now a successful oil executive. I can't.

I can tell you that Lance left Midland and ended up in Dallas, after stops in El Paso and Brownsville. His connections disappeared, and so did his options. Lance ended up living a life of poverty rather than a life of privilege.

How would I know? I talked to his son, a student at the University of Texas-Arlington. He's a full-time student and a part-time cashier at a gas station by the campus. Oil may run in his veins, but unlike his father, he's committed to college rather than connections. And he's not in school just to accumulate knowledge; he has big plans to do something productive with what he knows.

3. *Sometimes who you know really* does *matter.* Of course, there *are* times when the right connections can be helpful—when it comes to employment, for example. According to a two-year study by Stanford and Columbia Universities, job applicants who were referred to a company by an existing employee were much more

likely to be interviewed and hired by the company than were those who didn't have a contact on the "inside."[4] In addition, networking significantly magnifies a job-seeker's reach. According to the "90,000 Rule," since the average person knows three hundred people, and each of those people knows three hundred others, then an individual's circle of contacts can be as large as 90,000. Surely someone in that group knows of a job opening.[5]

Want another example? When you're face to face with Regis on *Who Wants to Be a Millionaire?* having the right person on the other end of the phone-a-friend lifeline can be the difference between a million dollars and a million regrets! This is definitely one of those times when *who* you know makes up for what you *don't* know.

Finally, I can think of one other situation when who you know is more important than what you know; and frankly, it's a connection that will make a difference both here on earth and for all eternity.

I am a Christ-follower. Over the past thirty years I have developed a relationship with Jesus that brings peace to my heart and purpose to my life. Some may see that relationship as a crutch; I see it more as a lifesaver. Scripture tells me that Jesus will never leave me or forsake me . . . ever. I'm on his mind first thing in the morning and last thing at night. He longs to spend time with me.

Scripture also says that Jesus left the comforts of heaven and lived here on earth for thirty-three years to model life for me . . . and then to die for me. No one took his life; he volunteered it. Someone had to pay the price for my sin, so Jesus raised his hand and became the sacrificial lamb. Just before he left he said, "In my Father's house are many mansions. . . . I go to prepare a place for you . . . that where I am, there you may be also" (John 14:2–4 NKJV).

Now here's the important part: *the key that unlocks the door to heaven is based on who I know—not what I know, what I have, or what I did.* I have earned two doctoral degrees; but when my life is over, they won't mean jack. The only thing that will matter is not what I know, but who I know: Jesus.

Discover this truth for yourself; then teach it to your kids. Many people say that when you die, "You can't take it with you." They're wrong: you can take your family and friends. Teach the ones you love this spiritual truth. Help them realize that while they're on earth, what they do with what they know matters most, but up in heaven it's all about who they know . . . and who knows them.

THE LIE
Don't Talk to Strangers — or You'll Be Sorry

THE MOST IMPORTANT THING TO REMEMBER IS—
DON'T EVER TALK TO STRANGERS.

Christopher Robin

We used to see their faces on milk cartons. Unfortunately, we don't drink enough milk.

Whatever happened to ten-year-old Bianca Lebron? On November 7, 2001, this four-foot-eleven, brown-eyed fifth grader was standing in front of her elementary school in Bridgeport, Connecticut, when a tan van approached. The driver told Bianca that her uncle wanted him to pick her up from school and meet him at the mall. She got in the van and was never seen again.[1]

Whatever happened to seven-year-old Alexis Patterson? On May 3, 2002, this forty-pound little girl was playing on the property of Hi-Mount School in Milwaukee, Wisconsin. She was wearing a red hooded jacket, purple shirt, blue jeans, white Nike tennis shoes, and carrying a Barbie book bag. She hasn't been seen since.[2]

Whatever happened to twelve-year-old Steven Kraft Jr.?

Around 7:00 p.m. on February 15, 2001, Steven was walking his two dogs near his home in Benton Township, Michigan, just as he had done a hundred times before. While his two dogs were found sometime later, this five-foot-two, green-eyed boy, wearing a Charlotte Hornets basketball jacket wasn't.[3]

Maybe their parents didn't tell them. Maybe they didn't understand. Maybe they weren't paying attention when Christopher Robin explained it:

> One day Christopher Robin was about to leave for grandma's house outside the Hundred-Acre Wood when Piglet asked, "Is-is it safe?"
>
> "Sure," said Christopher Robin, "and it feels great to go out on your own sometimes."
>
> "Not scary?" asked Piglet.
>
> "I *was* a little scared at first," said Christopher Robin. "But my mother wrote down the Stay-Safe-Rules for me. Once you know them, being on your own isn't scary at all."
>
> Christopher Robin continued, "The most important thing to remember is—don't ever talk to strangers."
>
> "You mean people who look strange?" asked Pooh.
>
> "Silly ole bear," said Christopher Robin, "a stranger is someone you don't know. Most of them are nice, but a few aren't."
>
> "How can we tell who's not nice?" asked Pooh.
>
> "We can't tell the difference between a good stranger and a bad stranger by looking at them," said Christopher Robin, "so we should never talk to *any* strangers."[4]

Now, if you can't trust Christopher Robin, who can you trust?

Mixed Messages

Like most parents, Jenni and I felt compelled to equip our kids with the rules and tools necessary to conquer the challenges they'd face on the turnpike to adulthood. Finding great wit and wisdom in Robert Fulgham's book *All I Really Need to Know I Learned in Kindergarten*,[5] we found creative ways to teach our kids to:

- Play fair

- Don't hit people

- Put things back where you found them

- Hold hands and stick together

- Look both ways and cross at the crosswalk

- Wash your hands before you eat

- Flush!

- Don't take things that aren't yours

- Never talk to strangers

Instructions were given, notes were taken, attitudes were adjusted, and, generally speaking, our world became a better place. However, we experienced setbacks when it came to the last two rules.

We discovered that our children's way around the rule "Don't take things that aren't yours" was to make everything theirs. One day when Jenni and I weren't looking, our kids banded together, unionized, got a lawyer, and developed the

"Six Principles of Possession." They went something like this:

1. If I saw it first, it's mine.

2. If it's in my hand, it's mine.

3. If I had it a while ago, it's mine.

4. If it's not in my hand but I like it, it's mine.

5. If it looks like something I might want, it's mine.

6. If you're playing with it and you put it down, it's mine . . . unless it's broken. Then it's yours.

The other rule that became a challenge was "Never talk to strangers." Shortly after being told this rule by one parent, it was contradicted by the other, saying, "I just met the nicest man at Blockbuster." It seemed that as soon as our kids were able to recite the rule, we rescinded it:

"Go ahead, tell Mrs. Curry your name."

"What do you say to the nice man who gave you that sucker?"

"Come on, Son, speak up. The cashier wants to know how old you are."

Soon the "Never talk to strangers" message plummeted from a rule to a principle to a concept . . . and a very confusing one at that. Frankly, it left our kids wondering, "Do you want me to be safe, or do you want me to be social?"

Stranger Danger

According to the National Center for Missing and Exploited Children, there are currently about 1.8 million missing children in America. A closer look at the numbers tells an interesting story:

- A total of 797,500 children were reported missing in 1999.

- About 535,300 of these were runaways.

- About 204,000 were abducted by family members.

- About 58,200 were abducted by nonfamily persons.[6]

- Only about 115 of the 58,200 nonfamily abductions were of the most serious nature (the child was kept overnight, held for ransom, or worse), and about 40 percent of these kids (46 in all) were never located, identified, or returned home alive.[7]

With this data in mind there are several important points to consider. First, about half a million runaways leave home each year because they believe that life on the streets will be better than life at home. Everybody knows that life on the streets is brutal, so one can only imagine what life at home must be like for these kids.

Second, many custodial parents live in a constant state of anxiety, fearing that a noncustodial parent will pick up their kids for visitation—and never return. Apparently, each year about 200,000 of these parents have good reason to be anxious.

Third, the 46 killed or never found during 1999 is a pretty small percentage of the total nonfamily abductions (less than one-tenth of 1 percent to be exact).

Of course, that small percentage is of little consolation to the parents of Bianca Lebron, Alexis Patterson, and Steven Kraft.

A Message in the Music and the Media

In 1965 Cher put to song what Sonny put to words in their hit single "Don't Talk to Strangers." Seventeen years later Rick Springfield wrote a song by the same name; it peaked at number two on the charts in May 1982. The following year hard-rock group Dio sang their version of "Don't Talk to Strangers"; and in 1998 a different song with a very similar title—"Don't Talk 2 Strangers"—was recorded by R&B artist Chaka Kahn. You'd think the music industry was trying to tell us something.

In 1994 the same message was translated to television in the psychological thriller *Don't Talk to Strangers*, featuring former James Bond actor Pierce Brosnan. In this story a young mother is horrified to realize that her disturbed ex-husband is secretly following her and her son as they make their way across the country to establish a new home—without him.

Obviously, "Don't talk to strangers" is a message that has been repeated often by parents, performers, and even Pooh— but it doesn't seem to be sinking in. On September 27, 1993, Oprah Winfrey turned on the cameras and let the evidence speak for itself. Oprah enlisted the help of child-safety advocate Ken Wooden and several mothers who were playing with their kids at a local suburban park. While each mother emphatically insisted that her child would never leave the park with a stranger, each one watched in horror from a distance as her youngster cheerfully followed Ken out of the park to look for his lost puppy. On average it took thirty-five seconds to lure each child away from the safety of the park and the proximity of the parent. Thirty-five seconds.[8]

The Problem's in the Principle

The "don't talk to strangers" instruction that most parents give their children is noble in principle. But there are three practical problems that make it one of those half-truths that can cause our Pinocchio noses to grow.

For one thing, the rule is often contradicted shortly after it's communicated. As we've already mentioned, when we encourage our kids to be civilized, we minimize the rule we've just verbalized. While a mom knows how to evaluate the appropriateness of her five-year-old's responding to the cashier at the grocery store when asked, "And how old are you, little guy?" her five-year-old is thinking, *This person is a stranger to me. Isn't that the kind of person Mom said I shouldn't talk to?*

Secondly, the "don't talk to strangers" rule was created in a day when almost everybody knew their neighbors. It was a time when friends and family remained close to home and relationships were firm and long-term. In today's mobile society we move so often—on average every six to seven years—that the people next-door rarely rise above stranger status. Almost everybody is a stranger. Does that mean we shouldn't talk to anyone?

Finally, the rule implies that children shouldn't talk to strangers because strangers are likely to harm them, while family and friends won't. It's called "stranger danger." Actually, the research says just the opposite. Almost four times as many children are abducted by family members as by nonfamily persons. Family, friends, and others who are familiar to us are typically ushered inside the gates of family protection and given a free pass to interact with our kids. Unfortunately, trust and access are two staples that every child predator has learned to take advantage of.

When Right Went Wrong

On Friday, June 17, 2005, eleven-year-old Brennan Hawkins was camping with his Boy Scout troop in Utah's Wasatch-Cache National Forest. While Brennan was climbing a rock, his best friend took off down a narrow dirt path toward the mess hall, shouting to Brennan to meet him there. Brennan never arrived.

The boy's disappearance was as bleak as it was baffling. Temperatures in the rugged mountains were known to fall into the forties, and thunderstorms were known to clean the face of a mountainside like soap on a washcloth. Brennan was dressed only in a long-sleeved T-shirt, shorts, and sneakers.

More than three thousand volunteers dropped their daily routines and brought horses, all-terrain vehicles, and hiking equipment to the search site. "I got kids," said Curtis Jones, 39, of Harrington, Utah, as if his two-hour drive towing a horse trailer to assist in the search needed no further explanation. "If it was my kid, I'd want everybody I could get."[9]

Volunteers searched Friday, Saturday, Sunday, and Monday. Most refused to give up, even though some became discouraged as each day passed and each coordinate was combed. Ten months earlier, eleven-year-old Boy Scout Garrett Bardsley had disappeared only fifteen miles away, and he was never found. Perhaps Brennan's fate would be the same.

> Brennan's mother never stopped praying.
> Her searching was best done on her knees.

On Tuesday the search ended when forty-three-year-old house painter Forrest Nunley found Brennan "standing in the middle of a trail" about five miles from where he was last seen.

It turns out that Brennan wasn't as much lost as he was hiding. When interviewed, Brennan told Sheriff Dave Edmunds that because his parents had told him to avoid strangers, he kept busy looking for places to hide from the very people who were determined to find him.

"His biggest fear . . . was that someone would steal him," his mother said apologetically.[10]

TRUTH OR CONSEQUENCES

Clearly, the "don't talk to strangers" rule needs some refining. Suggesting that "stranger means danger" is a vast over-generalization and is often contradicted in social settings. Furthermore, while it's safe to suggest that family and friends ensure a sanction of security, the fact is, family and friends are often the first suspects when kids are missing or molested. All strangers aren't harmful, and all family members aren't harmless.

THE TRUTH

Sometimes it's OK to talk to strangers (especially when your parents are by your side). But keep away from strange people—not simply unfamiliar people.

What should you tell your kids about "stranger danger"? Here are ten recommendations:

1. *Let your kids know that child abductions are rare in real life—* even though they are common in the movies and on TV.

However, just so they'll know how to handle themselves
if something goes wrong, you're going to give them some
rules to help.

2. *Assure your kids that if they are ever lost, you will look for
them and never stop looking for them until they are found.*
Abductors will attempt to convince kids that their
parents don't care for them any longer or have given up
on them.

3. *If your kids are old enough to understand the difference,
amend the rule "Never talk to strangers" to "Never talk to
strange people."* It's ironic, but if your children are ever
lost in public, the ability to talk to strangers is actually
the single greatest asset they have for finding their way
back to you.

4. *Teach your kids that if they ever get lost, they should ask a
woman with children for help.* As sexist as it sounds, the
truth is that women with children are less likely to be
child predators, and they are more likely to stick with
a lost child until the situation is resolved. Men, on the
other hand, are more likely to say, "The customer service
desk is that way. You can't miss it."

5. *Teach your kids that if someone is attempting to abduct them,
they should fall to the ground kicking and screaming, "This is
not my parent! This is not my parent!"*

6. *If your kids are old enough, teach them the concept of "relative
risk."* If they are walking down the street where they live,
they are in a relatively safe place; so if a stranger pulls up
in a car and tries to talk to them, more bad things than

good things could happen to them if they respond to the stranger. On the other hand, if they are lost in the woods, they are in a relatively unsafe place; so asking a stranger for help is the better decision.

7. *Teach your kids that if a stranger asks them for help, they must not help.* For example, if a stranger asks their help in finding a puppy or looking for something in a car, they should tell the person to find an adult who can help them. Explain to your kids that while it's OK for a child to ask a grownup for help, grownups shouldn't be asking children for help; they should be asking another grownup.

8. *Create a family "password."* Tell your kids that if an adult says he is there to pick them up for their mom or dad or because there's an emergency, they should ask the person for the family password. If the stranger doesn't know the password, they should refuse to go with him.

9. *Teach your kids that if they're home alone, they should say to someone on the phone, "My parents can't come to the phone right now. Can I take a message?"* Furthermore, they should never open the front door to a stranger.

10. *If your kids are old enough to travel into cyberspace on the World Wide Web, make sure they're safe.* Place the computer in a public area of the house (not a bedroom), install Internet filters that block unwanted material, and instruct your kids to never give out personal information (full name, age, address, phone number, school, etc.) to anyone. You guard the front door of your home from strangers; do the same when it comes to those who would enter it through the Internet.

The bottom line is that parents must protect their kids from strange people, not strangers. To tell kids, "Never talk to strangers," promotes a rule that's both puzzling and impractical. There are times when talking to strangers is both polite and socially appropriate. There may also be a time when talking to a stranger is lifesaving. Furthermore, there are many more good people in the world than bad people—more helpful people than harmful ones—and child abductions by noncustodial adults are rare. Given these realities, our goal must be to distinguish between strangers and strange people—and teach our children to do the same.

Maybe Christopher Robin should change his rule from "never talk to strangers" to "never talk to strange people." On the other hand, his only companions in the Hundred-Acre Wood are Piglet, Tigger, Eeyore, Kanga, Owl, Roo, and Winnie the Pooh. If he rules out talking to strange people, then he won't have many conversations, will he?

13

THE LIE

If You Have Talent, You're Bound to Go Far in Life

IT TOOK ME FIFTEEN YEARS TO DISCOVER THAT I HAD NO TALENT
FOR WRITING. BY THEN I WAS TOO FAMOUS TO QUIT.
Robert Benchley

They say its tough being talented, triumphant, and less than ten years old. I wouldn't know. But here are three who would.

A Beautiful Mind

Growing up in a small farming town in southwest Nebraska, eighteen-month-old Brandenn Bremmer demonstrated to his mother that he knew the alphabet—by pure accident. By age two he was reading and memorizing children's books; by age three he was playing the piano. At five he took an IQ test and scored 178—although he never actually finished the test. He was too bored. (Just to give you perspective, any score above 150 is labeled "genius.")

With an IQ more than twice his weight, Brandenn played Mozart from memory: the first-movement theme from *Eine Kleine Nachtmusik*. He went on to compose and record several songs. At age six, when most kids begin first grade, Brandenn began his first year of high school. He spoke at his high-school graduation at ten and entered college at eleven. At fourteen he told his mother that he wanted to become an anesthesiologist and attend medical school at the University of Nebraska.[1]

A Beautiful Machine

Former NFL football player and coach Marv Marinovich decided to create an athlete so mechanically perfected and so mentally prepared, he couldn't fail. What's more, he decided this beautiful machine was going to be his son.

Born on the 4th of July, 1969, Todd Marinovich was raised to become the perfect quarterback—a robo-QB. Stretching exercises as a toddler and strict workout regiments as a teenager were normal life for Todd. Fast food and soda drinks weren't allowed to touch his fingers or his lips, let alone reach his stomach. By age ten he already had a throwing coach, an exercise coach, and a nutrition coach.

In high school Todd racked up a national record of 9,194 passing yards, gaining him the 1987 All-U.S.A. Offensive Player of the Year Award. His decision to play college football at the University of Southern California was preordained: his dad had been co-captain of USC's 1962 national championship team. As a freshman, Todd led his team to the Rose Bowl. Later he entered the NFL and signed a $2.27 million contract with the Oakland Raiders, where his father had played and coached.[2]

A Beautiful Match

Robert Fischer was born in Chicago, Illinois, at the Michael Reese Hospital on the banks of Lake Michigan on March 9, 1943. Following his parents' divorce, two-year-old Robert moved with his mother and seven-year-old sister, Joan, to Brooklyn, New York. Four years later Robert and Joan learned how to play the game of chess with a set given to them as a present. So began the legend of Bobby Fischer.

At thirteen years of age, Bobby became the youngest National Junior Chess Champion in the United States. By fourteen he was the youngest Senior U.S. Champion, and by fifteen he became the youngest Grandmaster in the history of the game of chess.

His most famous match took place in 1972 in Reykjavik, Iceland: Fischer vs. Spassky, the U.S.A. vs. the U.S.S.R. When the dust cleared, Bobby had broken the Soviet domination of the World Chess Championship, becoming the first American to win the title by defeating Russian chess star Boris Spassky. Bobby's moves were brilliant; his manner was brazen. At age twenty-nine, Bobby Fischer became a national hero in America and was crowned "the world's greatest chess player."[3]

More about Brandenn, Todd, and Bobby later . . .

Talent: A Blessing or a Burden?

Talent—isn't it great? The list of gifted people throughout history seems endless. The seventeenth century had Pascal; the eighteenth century had Mozart; the nineteenth century had Picasso. Today in America about four million people have soared above the 130 mark on a standardized IQ test, qualifying them for the term "gifted" and putting them in the top 2 percent of the population. Between 800,000 to one million are under the age of eighteen.[4]

Giftedness comes in many styles and is recognized in many fields. Some gifted young people who skyrocketed to the top of their trades are:

- David Farragut (military): David entered the Navy as a midshipman during the American Civil War and was given his first ship to command at age twelve. He went on to become the first vice-admiral and first full Admiral of the United States Navy.[5]

- Murray Gell-Mann (physics): Murray taught himself calculus at age seven, entered Yale at fifteen, and received his PhD from the Massachusetts Institute of Technology at twenty. His work on the theory of elementary particles earned him the 1969 Nobel Prize in Physics.[6]

- Nadia Comaneci (sports): At age fourteen Nadia became the star of the 1976 Olympics in Montreal. She was the first gymnast to receive a perfect score of 10—a feat she went on to repeat six more times. Returning home with three gold medals, one silver medal, and one bronze medal, she was declared Hero of Socialist Labor in Romania.[7]

- Stevie Wonder (music): Blind from birth, Stevie became one of the most successful and well-known artists on the Motown label, with nine number one hits and album sales totaling more than seventy million units. He recorded his first number one hit, "Fingertips," at age thirteen.[8]

- Dakota Fanning (movies): Born in Conyers, Georgia, this A-list "tweenager" has played opposite Sean Penn in the movie *I Am Sam*, Denzel Washington in *Man on Fire*, Robert De Niro in *Hide and Seek*, and Tom Cruise in *War of the Worlds*. She's made a name for herself in Hollywood that most can't duplicate in a lifetime—and she's only twelve years old.[9]

Unfortunately, history demonstrates that while many brilliant young people have made it big, others have bombed. Each had incredible potential; but somewhere on the road to success things went wrong:

- Paul Charles Morphy was recognized as the world's first chess prodigy in the mid-nineteenth century. He learned the game when he was eight, and by age thirteen he had become one of the best chess players in America. Unfortunately, after a European chess tour at age twenty-one, Morphy returned home and announced the inconceivable: he was giving up chess. Morphy "died in 1884 a penniless recluse haunted by paranoid delusions."[10]

- Tracy Austin was a tennis phenom. At age fourteen she was the youngest player to enter Wimbledon and the U.S. Open. At sixteen she won the Open, and by eighteen she was ranked number one in the world of women's tennis. Unfortunately, while Tracy's schedule was full, her heart for the game was empty. She retired from tennis in 1982 at the age of twenty.[11]

- One of America's most famous American flame-outs was William James Sidis, who, at age eleven, became the youngest person ever to attend Harvard. His professor's proclamation that Sidis "would someday be the greatest mathematician of the century" propelled the adolescent into celebrity status. Unfortunately, the stress of success was insurmountable, and Sidis suffered a nervous breakdown during his teen years. He spent the next two decades in semiseclusion. He died in 1994 at the age 46 from a cerebral hemorrhage.[12]

Sure, it's great to be talented.
But talent alone isn't enough.

TRUTH OR CONSEQUENCES

I have a question for you. I just walked through the laundry room and noticed a Tide box the size of a fifty-five gallon drum beside the washer. With three teenagers in the house, our washing machine operates nonstop, 24-7. I find that amazing in light of the fact that in four years our son will be in college and he'll wash his clothes twice per semester—if he comes home that often. In any event, according to the packaging, Tide now contains an "oxybooster," which is a biodegradable surfactant with enzymes to make whites . . . umm . . . "white."

That's nice to know. Now I can sleep at night.

Here's my question: what does it take for these amazing ingredients in the box to live up to their potential? The answer: application and determination.

The same is true for our kids. Within each of our kids are amazing, God-given talents and gifts that may (or may not) reach their potential. The difference between the doers and the dreamers is application and determination. Talent alone won't take our kids to the promised land. Telling them, "If you have talent, you're bound to go far in life," is the equivalent of dropping dirty clothes next to the Tide box and expecting them to be clean in the morning.

THE TRUTH

Talent won't take anyone, anywhere, at any time — unless it's applied with purpose and perseverance.

If we don't teach our kids that success in life takes more than sheer talent, our kids will grow up to be sorely disappointed—and our noses will grow longer. All kids have talent (albeit some more than others), but talent doesn't predict success. Many talented individuals throughout history have crashed and burned. Not even a high IQ predicts success. The research literature consistently shows that a high IQ predicts only one thing: academic achievement. It's the application of talent, forged with purpose and perseverance, that turns a talent into a tool . . . and a tool into an instrument worthy of the Master's hands.

You don't have to be the sharpest knife in the drawer to recognize the fact that most of the rewards in life go to those at the finish line, not the starting line. Everyone with talent will start the race, but only those who run with purpose and perseverance will finish it. Talent provides the gas, purpose provides the goal, and perseverance provides the resolve to keep running despite hardships along the way. Purpose and perseverance take the Tide out of the box and turn its potential into productivity.

The Power of Purpose and Perseverance

If you're looking for a role model to help you demonstrate this truth to your kids, look no further than Bill Broadhurst. Bill wanted to be a runner in the worst way, but he had a problem. When he was young, he had surgery for a brain aneurysm that left him partially paralyzed. He struggled first to walk, then to jog, and finally to run . . . if you can call it running. He wasn't much to watch, but he was faithful. Several times a week Bill Broadhurst would lace up his sneakers and make his way around the track. Time wasn't important; his results were measured by the heart, not the clock.

One day Broadhurst heard that his hero, the famous marathon runner Bill Rogers was coming to town to run in a ten-kilometer charity race. For several years Broadhurst had dreamed of running a race with his hero. Now his pain had a purpose. Broadhurst was willing to do whatever it took to progress from dreaming to doing, so day by day he prepared. This was his opportunity to accomplish his ambition and define his destiny.

It was like offering the presidency to a pauper.
Sainthood to a scoundrel. A medical degree to a candy striper.

Finally the day came. On a misty July morning in 1981, twelve hundred runners were positioned at the starting line. The swift were stationed at the front, the feeble to the rear. Broadhurst held tightly to his dream. Soon he would be standing face to face with his hero—if not at the starting line, then 6.2 miles later at the finish line.

The gun went off. It was 9:04 a.m.

Rogers ran like a deer. Broadhurst ran more like a duck. He had to throw his stiff left leg forward and pivot as his right leg hit the ground. Before long it became obvious that the pack would leave Broadhurst in the dust. Most of the runners were soon out of sight.

But Broadhurst was not out of spirit.

As expected, Rogers finished the 6.2 mile race in just 29.5

minutes. Seasoned runners finished in thirty-five to forty minutes. The moderates took about fifty minutes; the mediocre needed about seventy minutes. A full ninety minutes into the race, the maimed were still marching.

Broadhurst pressed on. He had never run this far before, and it showed. His left side was numb. There was pain in every step, but purpose in every stride. Bill Broadhurst was not about to give up, give in, or go home—not until he finished the race.

By 10:55 a.m. the police had removed the barriers along the road, and the spectators had scattered. The event was history to most—but not to Broadhurst. In his mind he saw only the finish line. On the street he heard only sarcasm:

"Hey mister, they went that-a-way!"

Broadhurst pressed on.

"What's wrong, crip? Did you get lost?"

He pictured the prize, not the pain.

"Give it up, gimp. Call it a day."

The words didn't matter—Broadhurst had a mission.

Broadhurst heard it all that day. But step out of the story for a second, and let me ask you a question: What comments have you heard from the crowd lately?

At school your child failed the third grade.

You hear: "What kind of parent lets a child fail?"

At the bank your funds are running low.

You hear: "Nobody else has this kind of financial problems."

At home there is an empty chair at the supper table.

You hear: "He's never coming back, you know."

At work you're minimized by your manager.

> You hear: "Quit now before they fire you."

In the mirror you can't help but notice your weight.

> You hear: "You were in good shape before. What happened?"

At church your behavior in a certain circumstance doesn't match your beliefs.

> You hear: "And you call yourself a Christian?"

Maybe you've experienced nothing but an uphill battle on the road of life. You're running low on "positive thinking." You reason, *Surely there must be a way out of this wilderness—a place to find a cool cup of water.* In the meantime it feels like August in Arizona.

Back to the race . . .

Despite what he heard, Bill Broadhurst pressed on. The streets were jammed with cars, so he moved to the sidewalk and continued his course. The pain was unbearable. His body said, "Quit," but his spirit said, "Never!"

Suddenly the tide began to turn. Somehow the pedestrians on the sidewalk recognized his situation. They began to applaud this courageous warrior as if he represented a part of each of them—the part that wanted to stay the course when life got tough, but didn't. Applause was heard from their hands, then praise was heard from their lips:

"You can do it!"

"Keep going!"

"Don't give up now!"

His body was numb, but his resolve was strong. Circled by his newfound supporters, he came within sight of the end. While the finish line had been removed by the race organizers, his goal had long been defined in his mind.

Then, a miracle.

From an alley nearby, another circle of people emerged. At the center of this circle was Bill Rogers, wearing his gold medal. He had just returned from the awards ceremonies.

The two circles converged.
Pupil and professor came face to face.

Broadhurst collapsed into the arms of Bill Rogers at the finish line. Rogers was quick to recognize the significance of the situation. He placed his medal around the neck of the warrior and whispered into his ear, "You're the hero of this race. You deserve the medal."[13]

Bill Broadhurst didn't come to run a race. He came to finish it. Purpose got him to the starting line; perseverance got him to the finish line.

Now let me ask another question: What about you? Did you come to run a race, or did you come to finish it?

Pass It On

The real question swirling around the center of this chapter is this: since talent will only take your kids so far, how do you teach them purpose and perseverance so they can go the distance?

The answer is twofold:

1. *You model it.* As you run your own race in life, remember that your kids are watching you closely—and a principle

practiced is always more powerful than a principle preached. Whether you have a weight goal, a work goal, a quit-smoking goal, or a return-to-college goal, finish what you start, and practice what you preach. Whatever talent you have, find a way to use it and don't quit. Nothing will speak louder to your kids.

2. *You reward it.* Whether in school, on the soccer field, or at the supper table, recognize and reward your kids' completed tasks—not just their talents. Praise a finished season, not just a championship season. As we've said before, behavior that's rewarded is repeated. So if you want your kids to learn to apply perseverance and finish what they start, reward their effort; let others reward their performance.

Remember Brandenn Bremmer, Todd Marinovich, and Bobby Fischer? Each of them had a full plate of talent, but history tells us they could have used a side order of purpose and perseverance too. Brandenn Bremmer committed suicide on March 15, 2005, at the age of fourteen. Todd Marinovich's NFL career ended during his second year with the Oakland Raiders due to ongoing drug charges. Bobby Fischer has been living overseas for most of the past decade. If he returns to the United States, he will be welcomed at the airport by representatives of the Department of Treasury for violating United Nations sanctions by competing in a chess tournament in Yugoslavia in 1992. He faces up to ten years in prison and a $250,000 fine.

I'll take a pound of perseverance over a ton of talent any day.

14

THE LIE
It Doesn't Matter What
You Do in Life,
as Long as You're Happy

THE CONSTITUTION GIVES EVERY AMERICAN THE RIGHT TO PURSUE
HAPPINESS. AFTER MORE THAN TWO HUNDRED YEARS,
MOST OF US ARE ASKING, "HAVE WE FOUND IT YET?"

Angie and Dana are best friends. Both are smart, sociable, and seventeen. One has parents who value *pleasure*; the other has parents who value *purpose*.

As a young girl, Angie saw action on the soccer field, the softball field, the basketball court, and the tennis court. While successful in each, she quit them all. Not because her interest dwindled, not because her skills declined, not because her free time diminished—but simply because they weren't *fun* anymore. Her mother taught the theory, "If it's not fun, it's not for you." That led to four sports in four seasons. When the going got tough, Angie got going—to another activity.

Dana began playing soccer with Angie on the Camden Comets when they were both nine. Angie was clearly the more talented of the two and started every game. Dana usually began the game on the bench but found her way onto the field by the second half. Noticing the light in her eyes when the game was over, Dana's parents encouraged her to push on. "I know it's no fun sitting on the bench most of the time," her dad told her, "but I can see you improving with every game." In fact, the more Dana practiced, the more she played. By the end of the season, Angie moved on, but Dana moved up. The next year Dana took Angie's spot as starting right forward on the team.

Meanwhile, Angie turned her attention toward music. Just as in sports, her instructors noticed that she had talent. Angie took piano lessons for sixteen months, followed by clarinet and guitar lessons. Because of her potential, each instructor pleaded with her to continue. Unfortunately, Mom met Angie after every lesson to evaluate the "fun factor." As soon as Angie's pleasure turned to perseverance, her mother guided her to another option.

It's healthy for parents to view ages four through ten as the "trial years" for kids' activities. But nothing worth pursuing is going to be filled with nonstop merriment and jubilation. Unfortunately, Angie's mom put "play before purpose" when it came to everything her daughter was involved in—from sports activities to Sunday school. As a result Angie was well on her way to becoming what parenting expert Stacy DeBroff calls a "serial quitter."[1]

Fast forward to the present.

Angie and Dana are seventeen. Angie has played a little bit of soccer, a little bit of softball, a little bit of basketball, and a little bit of tennis. She knows a little bit about playing the piano, the clarinet, and the guitar. She has had the opportunity to develop many skills, but she has mastered none. Over the years she "began and bailed" on everything she tried. Mom's blessing was a given.

Dana, on the other hand, found her passion on the soccer

field. It wasn't easy, but each year she improved, and each year her playing time increased. This year Dana made the varsity soccer team at high school and plans to play "premier" soccer for her city during the summer. You'll find her mom and dad, just like most proud parents, cheering in the stands.

By the way, none in Dana's family ever attended school past the twelfth grade. That's why Dana and her parents see soccer as more than a sport—it's a ticket. Dana dreams that soccer will soon pave the way for her degree in sports psychology . . . free of charge. Score!

The Hunt for Happiness

Happiness. We seek it for ourselves; we crave it for our kids.

In a recent study designed to identify parental priorities, moms and dads around the world were asked what they wanted most for their kids. The results were revealing. While most Europeans chose "good health" for their offspring, and most parents from Japan desired "success" for theirs, the majority of American parents proudly declared, "I just want my kids to be happy."

Thomas Jefferson was so passionate about the pursuit of happiness that he inscribed it into the U.S. Constitution. In 1776 happiness went from being a good idea to being an inalienable American right.

**Don't get me wrong—happiness isn't a bad goal.
It's just not a great one.**

Some people say that happiness can be found with your face in the sun and your feet in the sand. Others say it's found in "the journey." The most recent research suggests that happiness is a state of mind that lies deep within us. It may not be easy to find there, but it's impossible to find anywhere else.

When I returned home from college following my sophomore year, I was a deeply troubled twenty-year-old kid. Dazed and confused, I sat paralyzed for hours. Time passed like sand through an hourglass. I was at the end of my rope.

This was serious business. Soon summer would be over. When I returned to school . . . I would have to pick a major! Seventy-three options—from accounting to zoology—all screamed, "Pick me." I could choose only one. I felt like a criminal with a quarter in hand, standing before a pay phone. One call. That's it. Make it count.

And so I turned to the one who knew me best, the one who got me through seventh grade and acne: my mom. After hours of conversation and speculation, it was finally time for her to deliver the goods and plot my vocational destination. Mom's response? Just like Sally Field in the movie *Steel Magnolias*, Mom said, "I just want you to be happy."

Could I get my quarter back?

When some moms say, "I just want you to be happy," what they really mean is, "Go to Harvard and become a doctor." Not my mom. She really meant what she said. What she also meant but didn't say was:

- "I don't want to put any pressure on you."

- "I'll love you no matter what you do in life."

- "I have confidence in you and your decision making."

- "I want you to do what you want to do, not what I want for you."

- "I know that no job (no matter what it offers) will make you 'happy.'"

- "I know that God will lead your life as long as you follow his path."

I commend my mom. With seven words she communicated her unconditional love for me and her unwavering faith in God. Mom wanted the best for me more than she wanted bragging rights for herself. She believed the details were just the details as long as she saw a smile on my face, sensed peace in my heart, and saw God's presence in my life. Mom cared more about the condition of my heart than the size of my paycheck.

Ironically, parents who *really* want their kids to be happy won't focus on happiness as a destination, and they won't try to chart their kids' course. Instead, they'll provide them with a compass and a few good coordinates.

TRUTH OR CONSEQUENCES

"Just as long as you're happy . . ."

I've caught myself saying it. Chances are, you have too. What parents don't want their kids to be happy? Not just a handful of happiness (like the kind that's found on Christmas morning) but a long-term, deep-seated, nonmedicated happiness that lasts a lifetime. That's what we want for our kids.

Here's the bottom line: happiness is not a goal, it's not a gift, and it's not a right. To define happiness to our kids in terms like these grows Pinocchio noses. And despite what some may claim, God isn't as interested in our happiness as much as he's interested in our holiness. Happiness isn't a destination, and it's not found in the journey. It grows from the inside out, but it's bred in our kids from the outside in.

THE TRUTH

Happiness isn't a right.
It's a by-product of chasing your dreams
and living your purpose.

During more than twenty-five years of private practice, I was invited into the private lives of both the burdened and the blessed. In the process I discovered that there *is* a place called "happiness." It is found by kids whose parents have taught them to pursue two goals: *something significant to do* and *something significant to dream*. Let's look more closely at each of these.

Something Significant to Do

Everyone is driven by something. For some it's the material: possessions, power, or prestige. For others it may be the emotional: acceptance, approval, safety, or security. But for those who experience happiness beyond their circumstances, it's usually something else: purpose.

Just ask Ashley.

Dick Machovec said that in 2004 his granddaughter told her family that she was going to do something "to make you proud of me." They had no idea what she had in mind. At the time, neither did she. Ashley was a widowed waitress—a single-parent mom who barely made ends meet. Her former husband had been stabbed four years earlier and died in her arms.

But life was about to change for Ashley Smith.

"March Madness" is a term that refers to the annual NCAA college basketball playoffs. It meant something entirely different for those who were living in Atlanta in March 2005. Fear was in the air. Four people had been murdered: a judge, a court reporter, a sheriff's deputy, and a federal agent. You could almost hear what four million Atlanta residents were collectively thinking: "If they weren't safe, then nobody is."

Earlier an e-mail had been sent to the sheriff's office by a worried mom who feared that if the verdict in her son's retrial for rape wasn't favorable, he would take someone's life. But thirty-three-year-old Brian Nichols didn't waste time waiting for the verdict. While on his way to the courtroom, the six-foot-two former linebacker overpowered a female sheriff's deputy, stole her revolver, and began exacting his revenge.

While emergency personnel attended to the wounded, Nichols fled downtown Atlanta and made his way to the northeast suburbs. He forced his way into Ashley Smith's home in the Bridgewater Apartments as she returned home from a local convenience store at 2 a.m. She had moved into the apartment just two days earlier.

While Nichols was there, something strange began to happen. Over the next several hours, Nichols's captive became his companion.

Ashley believed that she was made for a mission. For several weeks she had been digesting the bestseller *Purpose Driven Life* by Rick Warren. Ashley began to read to Nichols from the book. She began with chapter 33, page 257, right where she'd left off reading the day before. After she read the passage, Nichols asked her to repeat it.

Watch closely. Ashley was about to go fishing . . .

"The world defines greatness in terms of power, possessions, prestige, and position," she read. "If you can demand service from others, you've arrived."

The hook was set. The bait was taken. With a pistol in his pocket, Nichols was able to demand service from anybody.

Ashley continued: "Jesus, however, measured greatness in terms of service, not status."

Service? In Nichols's world, service was a sign of weakness, not greatness. He needed convincing. Ashley told Nichols that he was not an accident but was placed on this planet for a purpose. Nichols felt too hopeless to have a purpose. "Look into my eyes," he said. "I'm already dead."

Now it was time to land this fish.

"You're standing in front of me for a purpose," Ashley said. "It may be that your purpose is to get caught and go to prison and share the Word of God with the other prisoners there."

Something she said made sense. Within a few hours Brian Nichols waved a white T-shirt and surrendered to the police.[2]

This fish was out of the water and in the boat. Nichols's life had turned from being driven by a problem to being driven by a purpose.

What Ashley knew, and what Nichols discovered, can be taught to our kids. Here are the four points parents need to emphasize:

1. Purpose produces passion.

2. Passion produces meaning.

3. Meaning produces significance.

4. Significance defines our legacy.

For a preschooler, purpose can be found in being a teacher's helper. For a teenager, purpose can be found in a degree program that fulfills a calling rather than a career. For an adult, purpose can be found in turning a load of lumber into a home with Habitat for Humanity. The list is endless, but the clock is ticking. Help your kids define their purpose, and you'll help them find the first coordinate to a place called "happiness."

Something Significant to Dream

Dreams. While sleeping, the average person dreams every ninety minutes. Adults spend about one hundred minutes a night dreaming; babies dream more than five times that. For most of us, dreams during the night are hard to remember. But for many of us, dreams during the day are hard to develop. This concerns me most, because these are the dreams that make a difference.

He was born on January 15, 1929. He entered college at the age of fifteen, was an ordained minister at seventeen, and completed his PhD by twenty-six. He was described by many as determined, devoted, and diligent. But most of us know about him because he was a dreamer.

Martin Luther King Jr. shared his dream with America on August 28, 1963, in Washington, D.C. Four years later he told us about visiting the mountaintop and seeing the "promised land." The next day he became a permanent resident.

King wasn't the only daredevil dreamer. There were many who dreamed before him. Jacob had a dream about a stairway to heaven. God came to Solomon in a dream. Joseph was a dreamer with a coat of many colors. When he told his brothers about his dream, they plotted to kill him. (Maybe he should have kept that one to himself.)[3]

Now, I'm going to meddle for a moment. What about *your* dream? Not the one you had last night—the one you had last decade. "Oh," you say, "I've never really dared to dream. Dreams are for the naive, the pretty people, the financially fit, or the spiritual insiders." Or maybe you admit that you had a dream, but it died some time ago—because of a divorce, a financial failure, or because those around you failed to see your vision. A dream is a delicate thing. It can be shattered by the criticism of a parent, strangled by the sneer of a spouse, or crushed by the frown of a friend. It can be worn by worry or paralyzed by fear. Maybe you got discouraged and decided to quit. You concluded that life would be safer if you lowered your expectations and deserted your dreams. You're right. Life would be easier if you decided to never dream again. But here's the problem:

You were made for a mission.

Scripture says that God knew you before you were born. You were fearfully and wonderfully made. He has a plan for your life.[4] Have yesterday's dreams become today's nightmares? The apostle Paul knew that feeling. He conquered his fears with these words: "But one thing I do. Forgetting those things which are behind me and reaching forward to those things which are ahead, I press toward the goal" (Philippians 3:13–14 NKJV).

Never give up. Never give in.
Never let go. Never.

I have two suggestions for you to share with your kids:

1. *Dare to be driven by your dreams.* Some dreams will be shared; some will be secret. Set your dreams high enough so that they can't be realized unless God shows up. Give him room. Dare the impossible. Dream big. You may be just one dream away from a destiny created by the Divine. That's the first coordinate.

2. *Remind your kids that they were made for a mission.* God has a plan for their lives and a purpose for their birth. Help them to find their dream, and then fulfill their dream. Print the dream on a note card, and tape it to their mirror. Let them see it first thing in the morning and last thing at night. Help them put details to their dream—then help your dreamers become doers. That's the second coordinate necessary to find a place called "happiness."

Without purpose, life has no meaning. Without meaning, life has no significance. Without significance, life has no satisfaction. Chase happiness and you'll find emptiness. Chase purpose and you'll find happiness—and so much more.

My goal is to raise kids who are driven by a purpose and challenged by a dream. What about you?

By the way, remember Ashley Smith? Sharing the secrets of a purpose-driven life saved her life. Believing that his life had purpose, Brian Nichols surrendered to police and saved his life. Knowing the role that Ashley played in his capture, police gave her a $70,000 reward . . . and it saved her bank account.

15

THE LIE
It's Not Your Fault

PSYCHIATRY ENABLES US TO CORRECT OUR FAULTS
BY CONFESSING OUR PARENTS' SHORTCOMINGS.

Laurence J. Peter

Have you noticed lately that nothing seems to be anyone's personal fault? Stuff just happens to them.

My eighteen-year-old daughter, Brittany, tells me that when she's driving our car, there are times when it will speed down the highway on its own; mailboxes by the side of the road will jump out and knock the mirrors off the doors; and the gas tank will drain itself without telling the gas gauge. Funny . . . that never happens when I drive the car.

What's wrong with the cars we drive these days? We can put a man on the moon, but Detroit can't find an engineer worth his pocket protector to fix our defective automobiles. While all the top-notch engineers from MIT have been busy working on NASA's billion-dollar spacecraft, our 1999 bucket of bolts has no mirrors, no gas in the tank, and four speeding tickets!

According to Brittany, it's not *her* fault. Engineers didn't design the car properly, neighbors didn't install their mailboxes properly, and policemen didn't gauge her speed properly.

Oh, now I understand . . .

The Twinkie Defense

Brittany isn't the first to use the "it's not my fault" defense, and she won't be the last. Insurance companies advise drivers at the scene of an accident to "never admit responsibility" for a collision, no matter what. They want time to find a loophole before you do something stupid—like admit you took your eyes off the road because you saw a sign for a shoe sale and ran into the car in front of you.

It's hard to believe, but somehow tens of thousands of smokers missed the message from the U.S. surgeon general that "cigarette smoking has been found to cause cancer" written on the sides of cigarette packs. After being diagnosed with lung cancer, these smokers saw an oncologist—and then an attorney who told them, "It's not your fault." A jury agreed: judgment against the tobacco companies for $250 billion.

Seventy-nine-year-old Stella Liebeck pulled away from a McDonald's drive-through window in 1992 and accidentally spilled her hot coffee on her lap, burning her skin. She claimed that the coffee was too hot, so it wasn't her fault. A jury agreed. She was awarded $160,000 in compensatory damages and $2.7 million in punitive damages. McDonald's was liable because they made their "hot coffee" . . . um, hot.[1]

Caesar Barber of New York has been supersizing his fast-food meals for several years, but he claims he didn't realize the habit was supersizing his waistline and minimizing his lifeline. By 2002 he had suffered two heart attacks, so he decided to sue fast-food giants McDonald's, Burger King, Kentucky Fried Chicken, and Wendy's for making him health challenged and horizontally handicapped. Barber, an obese maintenance worker, wanted to bite the hand that fed him. After all, it wasn't his fault. According to Barber, it was "the advertisements that got me."[2]

Perhaps the most outrageous use of the "it's not my fault" defense was proposed by the attorney of former San Francisco city supervisor Dan White. While White admitted that he had voluntarily resigned from his position with the city, a few weeks later he reconsidered. On November 27, 1978, White climbed through a basement window at City Hall, walked upstairs to Mayor George Moscone's office, and demanded his old job back. When the mayor refused, White brandished a hand gun and shot him. Four times. After reloading, White walked into the office of another public official, Harvey Milk, and shot him. Five times.

His explanation? In legal circles it became known as the "Twinkie Defense." Psychiatrist Martin Blinder testified that White was suffering from "diminished capacity" because he was addicted to fast food and sugar-rich snacks. Blinder argued that increased sugar levels left White unable to control his behavior; therefore, he shouldn't be held responsible for his actions. A jury agreed. White was given a nominal sentence and was back on the streets in six years.[3]

Now, you may never find yourself in a criminal case, looking for a loophole; but you may want to keep a few defense strategies on the back burner just in case. Here are a few that might work if you find your legal back against the wall:

- "It's not my fault; I have low self-esteem."

- "It's not my fault; I went to a public school."

- "It's not my fault; I haven't had my coffee yet."

- "It's not my fault; my inner child made me do it."

- "It's not my fault; my parents made me this way."

- "It's not my fault; you need to be more accepting."

- "It's not my fault; I just haven't been the same since Elvis died."

Exceptions to the Rule

Smokers, fast-food patrons, and disgruntled government employees aren't the only ones who use the "It's not my fault" defense to avoid taking responsibility for their actions. We all have a tendency to want to pass the blame around—even when we know we're in the wrong. Sometimes, however, "It's not my fault" is the right message at the right time for the right reason.

It doesn't take long for parents to discover that most kids are self-centered, self-serving, and self-absorbed. Let there be no misunderstanding: when I say "most," I'm not talking "51 percent most"—I'm talking "99.9 percent most." All kids grow up with narcissistic tendencies, and that's OK, but healthy kids grow out of these tendencies between the ages of eight and eighteen. As their narcissism diminishes, they develop the ability to empathize (understand how other people feel) and to love (put other people first). Remain narcissistic, and they can do neither effectively. But it's this narcissism that mandates the message "It's not your fault" under the right circumstances.

Young children not only believe they reside at the center of the earth, but that the earth was designed for them, around them, and because of them. Unfortunately, when something unfavorable happens to them, they believe they must be responsible for it—because everything that happens around them is somehow connected to them. As a result many kids walk through life with groundless wounds that bruise their spirits.

Bruce Willis knows that feeling.

Released in 2000, Disney's movie *The Kid* is a story about Russell Duritz, a thirty-nine-year-old, wealthy but unhappy and unlikable image consultant (played by Willis). Success has come at a cost for Russell Duritz: he's immoral, he's unsociable, and he's fearful of spending the rest of his life alone. Duritz needs someone to show him how to be free from his fears. Fortunately for him, he gets a second chance at life when an eight-year-old version of himself, Rusty Duritz, mysteriously appears.

Both older Russell and younger Rusty travel to their childhood home, where Rusty learns the horrific news that his mother has died. The older Russell knows that he has carried the burden of guilt and shame over his mother's death since that day. He kneels, looks the younger version of himself in the face, and says, "It's not your fault." Instantly this phrase frees young Rusty from the poisonous pain that Russell carried his entire lifetime—pain that explained so many of the choices he'd made.

Four words. That's all it took to loose and to liberate. At the right time, with the right child, in the right situation, the words "It's not your fault" are the perfect medicine to heal a heavy heart that has been battered by:

- Sexual abuse: "It's not your fault that someone older than you decided to use you for his sexual pleasure. You didn't deserve it."

- The divorce of a parent: "It's not your fault that your

mother and father couldn't save their relationship. You didn't cause it."

- The addictions of a parent (alcohol, gambling, shopping, eating): "It's not your fault that your mom decided to medicate her problems rather than eradicate her problems. You didn't trigger it."

- The death of a family member, friend, or pet: "It's not your fault that all living things will die and that some will pass away before their time. You didn't hasten it."

- A physical disability: "It's not your fault that you were born in a body that has more physical limitations than other bodies. You didn't make it."

- A mental disorder: "It's not your fault that a cloud of depression will find you on a sunny day. You didn't imagine it."

- Bullying: "It's not your fault that some people will try to help themselves by hurting others. You didn't invite it."

A Message for the Messenger

There also are places and predicaments when the message needs to turn from "It's not your fault" to "It's not *my* fault"—from healing someone else's heart to freeing your own. Many moms (and some dads) have been caught in the grip of guilt because they've accepted blame for crimes they didn't commit. They walk through parenthood with crippled spirits because of a rebellious child, a wayward teen, a pregnant daughter, or a thoughtless spouse.

Perhaps you're one of those moms. Your heart is heavy. Life

feels like an uphill journey. I'm not suggesting that you throw remorse to the wind, but let me encourage you to gauge the degree of your guilt and make sure that the punishment fits the crime. When moms commit *themselves* to ten years of guilt for a minor infraction, while judges set murderers free because of a technicality, something needs to be reevaluated.

If you're wondering when your own freedom should be found with the phrase "It wasn't my fault," here are some sample situations:

- You were sexually assaulted in college, and you've always regretted what you wore that night. It wasn't your fault.

- Your son struggled with his grades in school because of a learning disability, and you always felt responsible in some way. It wasn't your fault.

- You gave birth to a daughter when your husband wanted a son. It was his contribution that determined the sex of the child. It wasn't your fault.

- You were never loved by your father, and you constantly wondered if it was because of something you did. It wasn't your fault.

- You were minimized by a boss who believed that good-looking blondes can't have any brains. It's not your fault.

- One of your adult children continues to make poor choices when it comes to relationships, finances, and employment. It's not your fault.

- You struggled with postpartum depression following the births of each of your children. It wasn't your fault.

- It rained at the family reunion, and you felt responsible because you set the date. Unless you're Mother Nature, it wasn't your fault.

Moms across America have burdened themselves with guilt. They pick up their guilt like pebbles on the ground. Soon there's a souvenir for every struggle.

First you hold it in one hand; then you need two. Soon your hands are full, so only a pocket will do. As guilt continues to grow, pebbles become stones. Pockets begin to bulge. Stones become rocks—a rock for every regret. Then only a sack will do. Slung over your shoulder, the weight begins to wear on your back. The sack becomes a burden that must be pulled behind you like a U-Haul.

Sorrow and shame will do that, you know.

Your friends tell you that everyone feels this way. Not very comforting. Your therapist tells you to examine each stone, analyze each rock. Informative—but when your hour is over, you pack up your sack and leave with most of what you came with. Lawyers tell you your crimes have few witnesses, and the charges will never stick. Legalists tell you to work off each disappointment with a deed. None has lightened the load.

Jesus said, "Come to me, all who are weary and heavy-laden, and I will give you rest" (Matthew 11:28). Rest is good, but it's relief that you want. Jesus offers that too. Relief comes from realizing that God is in control of your life and that you're not responsible for . . .

**what you didn't cause, what you didn't create,
what you can't control, or what you can't cure.**

TRUTH OR CONSEQUENCES

We've covered the exceptions; now it's time to cover the rule. I have an observation, an explanation, and a recommendation—but first, let's spell out the truth behind the lie:

THE TRUTH

Stuff happens. Sometimes it's not your fault—sometimes it is. When it is, take responsibility and expect consequences. When it isn't, offer compassion and extend grace.

Take a look around. We live in a land where kids are out of control. In the classroom they disregard the rules, demean the teacher, and defy the principal. On the athletic field they challenge the umpires and criticize the referees. Parents are ignored. Police and politicians are ridiculed. Authority figures are treated with contempt, and consequences for their behavior are nonexistent. When confronted with their crimes, they cry, "It's not my fault!"

It didn't use to be this way.

Take a look back. When I was young (BSB—"before seat belts"), I knew if I got in trouble at school, I would be in more trouble when I got home. No questions were asked, and no explanation would suffice: it *was* my fault. Nowadays, before children go back to school, their parents have called a lawyer from the ACLU. The turnaround took place during the 1960s and 1970s, when well-intentioned baby boomers turned their backs on the Bible and turned their attention toward Benjamin—Dr. Benjamin Spock. He recommended a family democracy, where everyone was entitled to freedom of expression and freedom of choice. Parents were encouraged to sit cross-legged in their defiant child's playpen and negotiate bedtimes and boundaries. Parenthood moved from dictatorship to default. Families moved from being spouse centered to being child centered. Kids went from being family members to being family managers.

Unfortunately, few checked to see if this model was sanctioned by Scripture. I checked. It isn't. And it doesn't have to stay this way.

Now take a look forward. I have a recommendation: We return to a model where personal responsibility is promoted. As parents, we hold every child responsible for every action. Good choices are rewarded; poor choices are reprimanded. No legal loopholes. No exemptions. No "Get Out of Jail Free" card. We return to being parents who develop kids of character rather than kids of comfort crying, "It's not my fault!"

Under this model, you have three options in response to your children's questionable behaviors:

1. *In some cases you tell your kids it's not their fault.* (We covered these cases earlier.)

2. *In some cases you recognize it doesn't matter whose fault it is.* Faultfinding doesn't matter as much as solution finding.

3. *In some cases you tell your kids it is their fault;* therefore, there will be consequences to fit the crime. That's how you turn reckless children into responsible children.

Remember our car—the runaway wreck that Brittany claimed would speed on its own, throw itself in front of mailboxes, and run out of gas without telling the fuel gauge? Well, I felt terrible for Brittany. After all, I was putting my daughter behind the wheel of an outlaw automobile, and I just couldn't sleep at night.

So last weekend I replaced it.

I replaced our car with something that was safe, reliable, and economical: a twenty-six-inch Schwinn bicycle. That's right . . . a bike. Not just any old bike; this is a seven-speed model with alloy wheels and a soft-spring saddle. Now Brittany has nothing to complain about. Not only can she get where she needs to go, she can stay under the speed limit in style: it's a Tornado Cruiser.

Funny how that fixed the car and her sense of personal responsibility.

There's a time to be fair, there's a time to be firm, and there's a time to be fun. Our kids are counting on us to know when to do which. Be a parent—don't let them down.

16

THE LIE
Of Course There's
a Santa Claus

I STOPPED BELIEVING IN SANTA CLAUS WHEN MY MOTHER
TOOK ME TO GO SEE HIM IN A DEPARTMENT STORE
AND HE ASKED FOR MY AUTOGRAPH.

Shirley Temple

M ommy, how does Santa deliver presents to all the kids in one night?"

"Um, it's a time-zone thing. I'll explain it when you're older."

"Mommy, how do reindeer fly?"

"Um, kind of like the space shuttle. They have booster rockets."

"Mommy, how does Santa get down the chimney if we don't have a fireplace?"

"Um, he has a special key that unlocks all front doors."

"Mommy, how come Santa looks different in every store?"

"Um, I think it's the lighting."

"Mommy, why didn't Santa bring me what I asked for?"

"Um, there was a shortage of parts at the factory."

"Mommy, why do we buy toys for poor kids at the homeless shelter? Doesn't Santa bring them presents?"

"Um, go ask your father."

"Mommy, is Santa Claus real?"

"Um . . ."

Is Christmas taxing your creative capabilities?

For many parents Christmas and Easter are the two holidays that have not only challenged their checkbooks but also their character. In Christian circles they've caused more controversy than *The Da Vinci Code*. What do we tell our kids about Santa and the Easter Bunny? Will leading our kids to believe they're factual today and fictional tomorrow affect our credibility as parents? If we tell our kids that Santa Claus is a character from a fourth-century saga, will we reduce the fun and fantasy of Christmas?

Is Santa Claus an innocent character encouraging childhood imagination and family tradition, or does he minimize Christ at Christmas and maximize materialism? Is the Easter Bunny a harmless way to keep the kids busy while Mom gets the ham in the oven, or is he a dangerous myth that reduces the impact of the Resurrection?

These questions became moot for a group of parents who sent their kids to Wednesday-morning Mass in Santa Fe Springs, California, in November of 2004. During the service, Reverend Ruben Rocha took the opportunity to inform the kids that Santa Claus doesn't really exist. Parents were outraged.

According to the *Pasadena Star-News*, when one child asked, "Who eats the milk and cookies left out for Santa?" like George Washington, Reverend Rocha couldn't tell a lie. He responded that it was probably good ol' Dad. (No wonder dads always put in a few extra hours at the gym after the holidays.) One of those cookie-consuming parents was Rick Martin. His five-year-old daughter was in church that Wednesday, and he wasn't amused.

"I believe some of the innocence has been taken out of her childhood, and I'm very upset," he complained. "After she got home, I tried to very gently find out what she was thinking about Christmas, and she said she still believes in it, but she doesn't believe in Santa Claus as an institution anymore. . . . Now my daughter doesn't believe in Santa Claus. She sees him, and she knows it's a costume. What happens when we go to the mall this year? It'll just be a costume to her."[1]

Now, it may just be me, but doesn't this story seem a bit ironic? Not that there's anything wrong with the residents of Santa Fe who don't want to be "Santa free"—but that Mr. Martin would like Rev. Rocha to maintain the fantasy of Santa, when his calling is to promote the reality of Christ. Should pastors use the pulpit to "out" childhood characters like Santa, the Easter Bunny, and the tooth fairy? Probably not. Should I expect the church to promote folklore that can't be found in Scripture? Probably not.

Bursting the Bubble

I have to be honest. In all my years as a therapist, I've never once concluded that the Santa Syndrome was at the heart of any psychiatric disorder I was treating. That being said, it's often a difficult day of discovery for kids when they first doubt the existence of Santa, typically between the ages of eight and ten:

> I remember finding one of my Christmas letters to Santa on top of the fridge (I loved climbing around in the kitchen). I knew it was something I shouldn't have seen, so I put it back where I found it and never told my parents. I stopped believing in Santa from that point on but couldn't tell

anyone, in case I'd get in trouble. I felt like I couldn't come clean, so I just wondered for a long time.

Randy

My brother-in-law is much younger than us (he was three when we got married) and held tightly to his belief in Santa Claus. When he was about nine, he was taking a fair bit of abuse at school for still believing. Finally he just asked flat out, "OK, I want to know the truth. Is he real or isn't he?" My in-laws broke the bad news. He was devastated. He had been defending St. Nick all these years against the unbelievers, and now he felt like a fool. The clincher for me, though, was the way his little nine-year-old brain processed this perceived betrayal. I can still hear him crying through his tears, "You told me Jesus was real, and I ain't seen him neither. Is he real?"

Cheryl

I know a family whose daughter was heartbroken when she found out there was no Santa. She broke down in tears and screamed at her parents for lying to her. I know that's probably rare, but it still makes me think.

Patti

I'm fifty-five years old now, but as the youngest of my family, my mother kept the secret of Santa from me until I was seven. At school I stood up for my belief and insisted to my other playmates that he was real and alive, and I could prove it with my Christmas gifts. It was a big disappointment when I insisted that my mother tell me the truth—and found out. I don't blame her for this; I have children of my own and know the dilemma. However, it did affect my conversion to Jesus. Even now when I am witnessing, I have flashbacks to that time in the playground, and my thoughts get very confused.

Steve

I don't have a child, so it's hard to say what I'm going to do. But I do remember that even when I was nine years old, my parents told me that Santa Claus was real. Shortly after that I found out the truth, and it hurt my feelings so badly to know that my parents lied to me and that they were never going to tell me the truth.

Rochelle

When I found out the truth, it affected me a lot. I thought my parents were incapable of lying to me about anything. I was wrong. I trusted them blindly and without question, but when I found out the truth, it hurt. I've never trusted anyone as much since then, which is a good thing, I guess. It's like a small introduction to the real world. Maybe every child should be lied to like this to teach them about the world we live in.

Matt

And finally, a letter to the jolly imposter himself:

Dear Santa,

I wanted to believe in you, I really did. But then you destroyed the most sacred trust I had—the trust between my mother and me. When I was seven, she shared with me the truth that you weren't really real. I was devastated. I grew up believing that you were out there, interested in me, worried about me. I thought you were real. Losing you was like losing a loved one. When the truth was told to me, I felt like a part of me died. Then I realized I wasn't mourning you, I was mourning the loss of trust that I had in my mother. After all, if you weren't real, then maybe she wasn't my real mom either. That's how much I loved you.

Laurie[2]

Ouch!

Good Santa, Bad Santa

Before we commit to a plan that either condemns or commends jolly St. Nick, let's take a look at what's good and what's not so good about this Christmas tradition.

In support of Santa, an argument can be made that children have the right to be children—to experience the wonder and magic of make-believe. Who among us didn't try to stay up on Christmas Eve, hoping to catch a glimpse of the celebrated Santa unloading his bag of blessings? Or the awe we felt as we inched closer down the two-mile line in the mall to sit on Santa's knee and stumble through our Christmas wish list? White beard. Blue eyes. Baritone voice. Gentle hands. It was our idealized grandfather in red pajamas and four-inch plastic belt.

Educator and family expert Carleton Kendrick believes that young children benefit from the enchantment that comes from Santa Claus and other age-old traditions and folklore.[3] Legendary author J. R. R. Tolkien (*The Hobbit*, The Lord of the Rings) would have agreed; he believed that myths and fairy tales are extremely valuable for enlivening kids' imaginations.[4] I'm sure he would have found no argument from friend and fellow fiction writer C. S. Lewis (The Chronicles of Narnia), who also wrote mythical stories that were Christian at their core.

Author Gary Grassl believes that a child who is encouraged to believe in Santa is a child who will eventually believe in the Savior.

Santa is a tangible, simplified God that paves the way to belief in an intangible, supernatural God.[5] Hmmm. It's a thought.

On the other hand, a case can be made that believing in Santa Claus is counterproductive to developing a child's faith in God. For example, consider the seemingly innocent song by Fred Coots and Henry Gillespie that we've been singing since 1934, "Santa Claus Is Coming to Town." This traditional Christmas ballad portrays Santa as having many of the attributes of God. He's omniscient ("He sees you when you're sleeping, he knows when you're awake"). He judges behavior ("He knows if you've been bad or good, so be good for goodness' sake"). He's omnipresent ("You better watch out . . . I'm telling you why: Santa Claus is coming to town"). How can Santa come to everybody's town unless he's able to be in more than one place at one time? And while he may not have his hands on the Book of Life, "He's making a list and checking it twice."

Kids have to wonder, who is this guy—God Jr.? If he's not, he must be the closest thing to God this side of heaven—after all, he lives forever, he flies through the air, he travels through time . . . and he gives stuff away. If that's not God to a kid, what is? Comparisons are inevitable, and confusion is probable.

Another argument against Santa stems from the fact that his message focuses on "presents for performance." Frankly, parents have rewarded kids for model behavior since Cain and Abel. But for those children who are "peak performers," what does it say about their behavior if their parents are penniless, and their presents under the tree are best described as meager to mediocre?

By far, the two most significant arguments for giving Santa the sack have to do with the way the Santa story impacts a parent-child relationship. The first involves credibility. Just as the letters shared earlier illustrate, many kids struggle with feelings of mistrust and betrayal once they find out they've been misled by Mom and Dad. Typically these are kids who have put a great deal of trust in their parents' word and have defended their parents' honor before their friends. The greater the trust, the greater the loss: "If my mom told me that Santa is real, then I don't care what you say . . . Santa is real."

Ouch!

The second argument has to do with modeling. How can parents spend eleven months of the year teaching their kids to tell the truth and then suspend the lesson between Thanksgiving and Christmas? What kind of example does that set? There's a principle in the field of psychology that goes like this: don't tell your kids something today that you'll have to "untell" them tomorrow. Nothing confuses kids more than mixed messages.

Truth or Consequences

Now that you're totally confused (Santa-full vs. Santa-free), let me suggest a solution that incorporates the wisdom I've learned in the textbooks and the common sense I've learned in the trenches. It takes into account a model of child development and incorporates the magic of make-believe. Best of all, it won't cost you the trust that forms the foundation of every parent-child relationship.

First, let me be a psychologist for a second. In the 1930s and 1940s a Swiss psychologist named Jean Piaget offered a model of child development that focused on the mental capacity of children and the sequential stages through which they progress. According to Piaget, children begin with a world based on senses (what they feel, see, touch, and taste) and move toward a world based on reason (concepts like morality, empathy, and problem solving). Children are able to perceive and process more complex issues as their brains develop—more specifically, as their frontal lobes develop. You might think of it in terms of maturity: *mental* maturity. First we crawl; then we walk. For more than fifty years nobody has contributed more to our understanding of how children think than Jean Piaget.

With this model in mind I suggest that we tell our kids the truth about Santa—in stages. We don't lie, but we do allow for "pretend," just as we do with Winnie the Pooh and Thomas the Tank Engine. The world of pretend stimulates a preschooler but is senseless to a high schooler. As our kids develop the ability to handle more complex concepts, we proceed from "seeing" Santa to the story of Santa. From the giving of gifts to the greatest Gift ever given. From the secular to the sacred.

THE TRUTH

Telling kids something today, only to untell it tomorrow, will cost you your credibility. It's better to tell your kids the truth about Santa . . . in stages.

What is appropriate to tell your children about Santa and Christmas? It depends on their ages and mental maturity. Let me be more specific:

1. *Two to three years old.* "We're going to go visit Santa today at the store and get your picture taken. He's such a nice man, and he has a story that began a long, long time

ago. A story is told that each Christmas he celebrates the birth of Baby Jesus by packing up his sleigh and traveling around the world giving presents to kids. Now he's probably going to ask you what you want for Christmas. What are you going to tell him?"

2. *Three to five years old.* "Some people say that Santa lives at the North Pole with Mrs. Santa, his elves, and his reindeer, including Rudolph. In fact, a story is told that on Christmas Eve he celebrates the birth of Jesus by gathering lots of toys into his sleigh and traveling to everybody's house to place the toys he has for us under the Christmas tree. What do you think about that story?

"Now let me tell you about a real event that happened years ago, when God decided to give the very best gift he had and put it in a manger. It's the true story of the birth of Jesus . . ."

3. *Five to eight years old.* "Have you noticed that each store we go into tries to find a look-alike Santa? That's because the real Santa, St. Nicholas, lived in a country called Turkey hundreds of years ago. He was a priest and a wealthy man who helped poor kids by giving them gifts each Christmas. Well, St. Nicholas didn't want anyone to find out who he was, so the kids were told to go to sleep first, and that began the tradition of putting gifts under the tree after all the kids are in bed.

"St. Nicholas was inspired by Jesus. Jesus was born at Christmastime to show us the way to have a relationship with God. Jesus ended up giving the best gift of all—his life—so that one day we could go to heaven. Jesus teaches us that we should give gifts to others who are less fortunate than we are. Let's find a gift for someone else this year . . ."

4. *Eight to ten years old.* "What do you think about the story of St. Nicholas and why he gave gifts to kids at Christmastime? Do you know the real meaning of Christmas and why we give gifts to one another? Let's talk about the gift that God gave us and what Jesus taught us about living for God. Maybe this would be a good time for us to do what St. Nicholas did and celebrate Christmas by giving gifts to those who are less fortunate than we are. Who do you think Jesus would want us to help this Christmas?" . . . "That's a great idea . . ."

Answer specific questions about Santa with specific, developmentally appropriate answers. Talk about "the story" of Santa. Use terms like "a long, long time ago, a story is told . . ." Later, connect the story of Santa to the legend of St. Nicholas, and eventually connect the gift giving of St. Nicholas to the reason behind the season: the greatest gift of all, Jesus. Finally, guide your child's heart from "What will I get?" to "What can I give?" thereby keeping the spirit of Christmas alive for others.

Remember that while all kids will pass predictably through the classic stages of mental maturity proposed by Piaget, they will do so at different speeds. The age guidelines I've suggested are general. Let your children's questions tell you which stages they're at with their Santa suspicions. I don't see a need to push those kids who want to hold on to the traditions of Santa a little longer. Nor do I see a need to prolong the traditions for those who want to move ahead a little faster.

To Santa or not to Santa . . . this is the question.
I say the answer is simple:
"yes" to both.

THE LIE

Busy Kids Are Happy Kids

IF BUSYNESS IS NEXT TO GODLINESS,
THEN MOST OF OUR KIDS ARE DESTINED FOR SAINTHOOD.

W hen the school bell rings at the end of the day, almost 70 percent of America's teens say they're "ready to go home, take it easy, do homework, and spend some time with friends." Unfortunately, for almost 80 percent of all middle-school and high-school kids, their day is just beginning. It will include soccer, baseball, tennis, ballet, basketball, football, drama club, band, cheerleading, debate team, gymnastics, lacrosse, church, dance class, Scouts, tennis lessons, figure skating, piano lessons, tae kwan do, yearbook—and *then* homework. For 57 percent, this level of activity will be a daily ritual.[1]

Meet Melissa. She lives in Henderson, Nevada. Melissa has been taking gymnastic lessons for the past two and a half years. She is also involved in baseball, tennis, and soccer. During the summer she fills her days with swimming classes. To help broaden her extracurricular activities, Melissa's parents have enrolled her in weekly piano lessons that require daily practice.

Melissa also attends Daisy Girl Scouts, which is the entry level of Girl Scouting.

Melissa is five years old.[2]

Meet Tate. When he was seven, Tate showed great promise with the puck and started playing hockey for his town's youth hockey program in New Jersey. Tate is twelve now, but most people describe him as an unbelievable hockey player. He's a member of the county all-star team and plays competitive hockey twelve months a year. Tate has four practices a week. Most are early morning ice times. Games are on weekends. Next year his coach wants him to "kick it up a notch," so he's scheduled to practice six days a week.[3] Progress has a price tag.

Now meet the parents. Melissa's mom, Katie Jones, is described as loving, committed, and concerned about her daughter's long-term success. She views Melissa's activities as tools that will shape her into a well-rounded, versatile girl. She believes that "kids thrive when challenged" and admits that her daughter would "be in more activities, if I had more time." It's no surprise that thirty-two-year-old Katie admits she felt left out when she was a child because she didn't participate in any organized activities.[4]

Tate's dad, on the other hand, was an avid athlete and a former prep-school hockey star. At first he taught Tate how to skate—then enrolled him in formal lessons a few months later. Tate was two years old. Today his mom, Elaine, says, "I really enjoy watching him play." But that's not the only reason she's at all of her son's games. "He still needs me to tie his skates for him," she says.[5]

If idle minds are the devil's workshop,
then Melissa and Tate have nothing but heaven ahead of them.

They're not alone:

"She's not really good at soccer, and she doesn't really like to play; but all her friends are doing it, and if she doesn't play, she'll be left behind," reports the mother of a nine-year-old.

"If I miss a practice, even for a doctor's appointment, I get benched, and my teammates think I'm slacking off," a thirteen-year-old says.

"I don't really like lacrosse, but I play because it'll look good on my college transcript," a sixteen-year-old explains.

"If my son didn't have an after-school activity every day of the week, he'd sit around eating junk food and playing video games," declares the concerned father of a ten-year-old.

"She wants to take gymnastics, art, dance, and cooking, and she goes to afternoon religious classes twice a week. I'm not pushing her, honest. She has to eliminate something!" exclaims the exhausted mother of a seven-year-old.

"I don't have anything scheduled on Sunday afternoons. That's when I have my life," a fourteen-year-old reasons.

Does anyone see a problem with this picture?

Trophy Kids

Not so long ago, kids had time on their hands—and it was considered a good thing. After school they'd sneak a few cookies from the kitchen and sprint out the door to play with their pals. On Saturdays boys would ride bikes and build forts in the forest. Parents were lucky if the kids returned home to grab a sandwich before heading out the door again to hunt down a few harmless garter snakes. Girls got together by midmorning to play with Barbie dolls in their bedrooms or dress up in the attic. Today such activities are practically unheard of.

Author David Elkind warned us about the belief that "busy is better" twenty years ago in his book *The Hurried Child: Growing Up Too Fast Too Soon.*[6] He predicted that the growing trend to create "superkids" by scheduling a dizzying number of activities from dawn to dusk would rob them of their childhood. He was right. Today well-intentioned parents are busy raising "Renaissance kids."

But I thought childhood was designed to be
preparation time, not performance time.

Recently Matt, Katie, and Al tackled this issue on NBC's *Today Show.* The guest on the program was child psychiatrist Dr. Alvin Rosenfeld, author of *The Over-Scheduled Child: Avoiding the Hyper-Parenting Trap.* Matt began the interview by noting that after surveying 14,000 parents, *Parenting* magazine found that 86 percent of them thought their kids were overscheduled. Dr. Rosenfeld responded by stating that kids have 100 percent more scheduled activities and 50 percent less free time than they had just twenty years ago. He summed up the situation with this telling statement: "Golf is no longer America's most competitive adult sport; parenting is."

His solution? Downtime. And if you want to get involved in your child's downtime . . . do nothing with them. That's right—nothing. "Nothing enriches a child more than just spending time with them with no goal in mind other than pleasure. My happiest memories are on a fishing boat with my dad when we did nothing particular, just sat together," Dr. Rosenfeld said.[7]

Barbara Coloroso, author of the best-selling book *Kids Are Worth It*, agrees with Dr. Rosenfeld about the importance of downtime. She concludes that parents minimize its value because they don't feel comfortable being alone themselves, and they project their feelings onto their kids. Coloroso says, "If a child is daydreaming or likes to go on long walks alone, they're encouraged to find something to do with someone. If a teenager wants to spend time alone in his room, he's called 'antisocial'."[8]

In reality many of the luxuries we enjoy today were developed by "creative tinkerers" who had time on their hands. They had time to think creatively and explore the possibilities of their thoughts. Nowadays Albert Einstein would have to develop the theory of relativity in the back seat of a minivan between piano lessons and gymnastics!

Maybe it's just another middle-class malady. That's what Robert Glossop from Ottawa's Vanier Institute of the Family concludes. He identifies the overscheduled child as a middle- to upper-middle-class phenomenon, stating, "These parents are well-intentioned parents who want to give their children opportunities that they had"—like Tate's dad—"or in some cases, didn't have"—like Melissa's mom—"when they were growing up." These parents believe that organized activities give children a leg up in an increasingly competitive global society. "That's why you hear of eight-year-olds taking investment counseling or attending computer camps," Glossop explains.[9]

A twelve-year-old without a pocket protector or a PDA?
What's this world coming to?

Revising Our Rationale

There's no question that overscheduling parents are well-intentioned parents. There are many reasons for signing up our children for a full plate of extracurricular activities. Let's take a look at two of the most common.

The first reason suggests that if we withhold any of the count-less activities *du jour* from our children's menu of extracurricular options, we put our kids at a competitive disadvantage next to their overprepared peers. If little Missy is going to impress the admissions counselor and climb the Ivy League vine, she'll have to spend her summers at space camp, take six years of Greek, play varsity basketball, volunteer as a candy striper at the hospi-tal, and score 1500 on the SAT. If not . . . say hello to the local community college. Right?

Actually, times may be changing. Marilee Jones, dean of admissions at the Massachusetts Institute of Technology, agrees that kids are overscheduled and decided to do something about it. In 2002 the average MIT wannabe listed twelve extracurricular activities on his or her admission application. In an attempt to separate solid students from activity automatons, MIT began asking students to explain what they did for fun. That's right—fun. Jones estimates that about fifty students admitted for the fall 2004 semester made the cut because of the new criteria.

The new application for 2005 allows only five lines for listing extracurricular activities (down from ten). Instead, MIT admissions counselors are reading about applicants who make smoothies trying different concoctions, watch classic movies with their moms, and ground telescope lenses in their basements because they love looking at the stars. These kinds of kids are "a great fit for us," Jones says.[10] Today more and more schools like MIT are looking for BWRKs—bright, well-rounded kids, not just busy kids.

The second reason parents overschedule their kids goes like this: if we start our kids in an activity early in life, they will be much better prepared and more proficient at the skill involved than their peers who start later. If little Ryan isn't in Little

League by age five, everyone will live to regret it by the time he turns ten. After all, earlier means better. Right?

Actually, a walk around the average home in America will reveal hockey skates gathering dust in the basement, an electric piano sitting silent in the family room, or an oversized tennis racket languishing in the corner of the closet. Yesterday's focus of involvement has becomes today's featured item for the garage sale. Unbridled enthusiasm degenerates into an unremitting test of endurance. After four years on a select team, three summer camps, and untold miles on the minivan, Junior announces, "I don't want to play. It's just not my thing anymore."

It's called the "fadeout factor."

Stacy DeBroff, author of *Sign Me Up*, notes that while a small percentage of kids are "serial quitters," the years between four and ten are "the trial years." She expects most kids by age ten to have had at least seven activities that they loved then left. As their energy levels, interests, and friends change, so will their dedication to certain extracurricular activities.[11]

Not to worry; there's no evidence that a lack of "activity breadth" will cost a child "activity depth." Richard Stratton, associate professor of health promotion and physical education at Virginia Tech states, "There is no evidence of a long-term value to starting [a sport] early. Kids reach their optimal performance level in most activities late in high school. There is no advantage to starting at six or seven if a child will be tired of the sport by the time he reaches his physical capability."[12] In other words, we can start our children in a sport at age five, but the chances that they'll still be in the same sport thirteen years later, when they reach their optimal performance level, are slim to slimmer. Those who start a sport early . . . typically quit early.

TRUTH OR CONSEQUENCES

To be fair, extracurricular activities are not the problem. As Maureen Weiss of the University of Oregon and other researchers have discovered, children who are involved in extracurricular activities reap significant benefits. Involvement in athletics, for example, correlates with increased self-confidence, improved academic performance, fewer behavioral problems, and a lower likelihood of drug involvement and sexual activity.[13] According to a study by the Department of Health and Human Services, students who spent little or no time in extracurricular activities were 57 percent more likely to have dropped out of school by the time they would have been seniors; 49 percent more likely to have used drugs; 37 percent more likely to have become teen parents; 35 percent more likely to have smoked cigarettes; and 27 percent more likely to have been arrested than those who spent one to four hours per week in extracurricular activities.[14]

Clearly, some extracurricular activity is good for kids. The uninvolved tend to underachieve. The question is: how much extracurricular activity is healthy? The answer can be found in the words of the greatest overachiever of all time: "To everything there is a season" (Ecclesiastes 3:1 NKJV). Solomon's solution is simple: strive for balance.

THE TRUTH

Busy is not better . . .
it leads to overwhelmed kids
and overspent parents. Balance is better.

Benefits are abundant for the involved, but consequences abound for the overinvolved, including stress, anxiety, sleeplessness, fatigue, apathy, decreased concentration, and lost family time.[15] I don't know if Solomon struggled with an onslaught of extracurricular activities, but his solution is suitable for all of us living in the twenty-first century: moderation. Here are some ideas on how to add some balance and quality to your child's life.

1. *Set aside quality family time.* As a Psychiatrist, Rosenfeld came up with his own solution to the problem of too-busy kids. He introduced America to National Family Night, and the word is spreading. Parents are encouraged to set aside one night per year for family activities. The agenda may be as simple as doing nothing together. Rosenfeld's goal is to move National Family Night from an annual event to a monthly event.

   Inspired by Dr. Rosenfeld the entire town of Ridgewood, New Jersey, decided to give Family Night a try. With support from school teachers, administrators, and religious leaders, the town cancelled all sports activities, homework assignments, and even religious events so families could spend time together on March 26, 2002. Ninety-one percent of Ridgewood families participated. The town has repeated the event every year since.[16] A similar program called Family Life First has been tried in Minnesota with positive results.[17] Some families set aside one night a week as family night. Whatever works for your family, time spent together won't happen by itself; you, as the parent, must make intentional plans.

2. *When necessary, step in and help your kids trim their schedules.* Sometimes, though, change needs to be more immediate and more dramatic. Exhibit A: Jessica. Eight-year-old Jessica was exhausted—for good reason. Her schedule was filled with dance, ice skating, piano lessons, swim team, and soccer. "When the headaches started, that was the last straw," her concerned mom said. She pulled Jessica out of everything. Later, when Jessica felt better, she chose one activity: swim team. "She's a normal kid again, and we actually have time to be a family again," Mom beams.[18]

The fact is, busy kids are not necessarily happy kids. Many, like Jessica, are simply worn out after fourteen-hour days filled with school, sports, and self-improvement activities.

A recent issue of *Time*, dedicated to the challenges of being thirteen, included stories of self-motivated kids like Katherine Rack. Katherine's schedule includes cross-country, track, gymnastics, piano, and drama. She's also a straight-A student. But Katherine admits, "One of my greatest struggles is trying to find time to spend with my family and friends on top of all my activities. . . . I also long for the nights when I used to relax with my family. Now I come home from meets and practices to eat and finish homework. Many times I am exhausted."[19]

Kids like Katherine are definitely going places, but they may be short of fuel, friends, and family when they get there. Others, like five-year-old Melissa and twelve-year-old Tate—by-products of well-intentioned parents—are likely to meet a similar fate.

Slow down! Your daughter will get into college without listing six pages of extracurricular activities. Your son won't fall behind athletically because you didn't strap skates on his feet the day he started walking. Research continues to confirm that the healthiest and happiest kids on the block are the ones who are rich in relationships—especially with their parents. Believe me, there is an upside to downtime!

By the way, if you're wondering how Jenni and I handle the busy-kid syndrome, I can tell you we've been guided by one rule and one routine.

The rule: one activity per child per semester. (Choose wisely.)

The routine: Jenni is the keeper of the calendar, and she bends over backward to juggle supper times so we can eat together as a family.

These two principles have proven to be healthy for our kids . . . and heaven for their parents.

THE LIE

All Good Things Come in Small Packages

MANY A SMALL THING HAS BEEN MADE BIG BY THE
RIGHT KIND OF ADVERTISING.

Mark Twain

"All good things come in small packages"—that was the mantra heard from the delivery room at Loyola University Medical Center on September 19, 2004.

Described as being as small as a cell phone, Rumaisa Rahman was born weighing only 8.6 ounces. She is the world's smallest known surviving baby, nudging out the previous record setter by 1.3 ounces. Her twin sister, Hiba, who weighed a whopping 20 ounces, was more than twice Rumaisa's size. Their parents, Mohammed and Mohajabeen Rahman from Hanover Park, Illinois, were elated by the birth of their first children. "It's a blessing, it's a great blessing," Mom said following the delivery.[1]

> Rumaisa may be small in size, but that's OK.
> "Small" is the new "big."

Nine-year-old Sara Webster is small in stature, but she's proven that even at three-foot-eleven and forty-seven pounds, she can play with the big boys . . . literally. Sara is a fourth grader at Englewood Elementary School in Englewood, Florida, yet she plays soccer like a seasoned veteran. According to her coach, Jeff Wiederspiel, Sara's size is on her side. "She catches people by surprise," he says. "She is a tiny little girl who is quick and can dribble the ball extremely well. She outmaneuvers most of the people who are twice her size." On the soccer field she is described as "quick" and "elusive." Both attributes are made better because of her stature—or lack of it.

Incidentally, most of the players that Sara competes against are twice her size for good reason—they're guys. Sara has played nearly all of her soccer against boys. She grew up in the Cayman Islands, where soccer is more of a religion than a sport. She played on the all-boys school team there at age six. Three years later she was asked to play on the Cayman Islands' Boys National Team.

By the time her family moved to Englewood, Florida, her skill level had grown way beyond her size level. She was the top female player on her predominately male Englewood Youth Soccer League team and was selected to play on the mixed-gender All-Star Team in statewide tournaments.[2] Remember, she's less than four feet tall! Do yourself a favor and make note of the name Sara Webster. Someday you'll hear it slide off the tongue of a sports announcer. This little soccer star is on her way to celebrity status. She's taken the old adage "all good things come in small packages" to a new level.

Want another example? Towering taller than his five-foot-seven body would suggest, Spud Webb made his living in the land of the giants, playing twelve years in the National Basketball Association. In 1986 he became the shortest player in history to ever win the NBA Slam Dunk Contest. There's no question about it: this basketball superstar was a good thing in a small package. He wasn't the only NBA player to fit that description.

At only six feet tall and 165 pounds soaking wet, Allen Iverson of the Philadelphia 76ers became the shortest and the lightest NBA player to win the league's Most Valuable Player Award. Seven-foot-one Shaquille O'Neil won the MVP in 2000, and six-foot-eleven Tim Duncan won it in 2002. But in 2001, while playing against these "twin towers," Iverson led the league in scoring (thirty-one points per game) and minutes played per game (forty-two).

For Sarah Webster, Spud Webb, and Allen Iverson, "big" describes the size of their game, not the size of their frames.

Of course, these three aren't the only undersized celebrities who have supersized their performance. Take a look around. There's plenty of talent tucked away in small packages:

Psychotherapist Dr. Ruth Westheimer .... 4'7"
Actor Gary Coleman.. 4'8"
Gymnast Mary Lou Retton.. 4'9"
Mother Teresa.. 4'10"
Joan of Arc... 4'11"
Singer Dolly Parton .... 5'0"
Saint Francis of Assisi... 5'1"
Actress Sally Field .... 5'2"
Mahatma Gandhi .... 5'3"
Artist Pablo Picasso .... 5'4"
Magician Harry Houdini .... 5'5"
Actor Dustin Hoffman .... 5'6"

But forget fame for a moment. Let's talk fortune. In the corporate world, "big" used to be better. "Big" meant more products at less cost, which equaled big profits. It meant added value because of employee efficiency and cost-cutting clout. Megastores offered more variety than mom-and-pop shops. SUVs were deemed safer than subcompacts. Big homes, big lots, big cars—"big" became the definition of someone who had arrived.

Then "small" happened.

People began to realize that megastores are impersonal. SUVs are gas hogs that tend to roll over in accidents. Big homes on big lots with big cars in the driveway . . . come with big payments.

Nanotechnology began to drive the economy. Boom boxes were replaced by iPods. Laptops became smaller than lunchboxes, and cell phones became the size of credit cards.

Enron (big energy firm) got audited by Arthur Andersen (big accounting firm), and both failed big time. Big airlines like Northwest are getting their wings pinned back each year by smaller competitors like Southwest. American, the largest airline, is being outperformed annually by Jet Blue, one of the smallest. With gas prices rising, Honda is replacing HUMMER as America's vehicle of choice. The new clarion call of the successful has become, "Think big. Get small."

"Small" is the new "big." But wait—there's a catch.
It all depends on what you're measuring.

TRUTH OR CONSEQUENCES

Sit at the feet of three-foot-eleven inch Sara Webster for a few seconds. Quickly you discover that the only thing small about

Sara is the size of her body—not the size of her dreams. On the outside she may be a bantamweight, but on the inside she dreams like a heavyweight. "Someday I want to be a famous soccer player and play against the men," she says. "When that happens, I want to be sponsored by Nike, because they give you a lot of money and free shoes and stuff."[3] Um, Nike better set aside a size three!

Our kids need dreams the size of Sara's. They need to dream *big*.

THE TRUTH

Some good things in life *do* come in small packages; but when it comes to the size of our dreams, bigger is better.

Small dreams produce small dividends. Big dreams birth a big destiny. As parents we need to feed the ambitions of our kids to go not only further than they've ever been before, but further than they've ever dreamed before.

In order to transform your child into a big dreamer, first you may need to dream big yourself. So let me encourage you to pack your bags and travel with me from the Land of the Familiar to the Land of the Possibility. Shortly after you arrive, you will experience an amazing transformation that occurs deep within the heart of a dreamer. Here's a synopsis of how my personal friend, best-selling author Bruce Wilkinson, tells it in his profound story *The Dream Giver*.

Not long ago and not far away, a nobody named Ordinary

lived in the Land of the Familiar. Every day was pretty much the same for Ordinary: get up, work, eat, watch TV, go to bed, repeat. Ordinary thought he was content. His routines were reliable, his worries were minimal; his life was comfortable.

Then one day Ordinary noticed a small, nagging feeling inside that seemed to tell him something big was missing in his life. The feeling—one that few in the Land of the Familiar ever experienced—grew. Some time later Ordinary heard these words: "What you're missing, you already have."

Ordinary looked and looked for the source of the statement. Finally he discovered that in the corner of his heart lay a Big Dream. The Big Dream told him that he, a nobody, was made to be a Somebody and to achieve Great Things.

The Big Dream had come to Ordinary from someone known as the Dream Giver. While Ordinary had heard rumors of the Dream Giver and of Big Dreams coming to others, he had never imagined that such a thing would happen to him.

At first Ordinary kept his Big Dream to himself, fearing he would become the town fool if he shared it. Eventually, though, he told his dream to his best friend—who predictably suggested that Ordinary keep quiet about it. Big Dreams weren't a part of life in the Land of the Familiar.

Discontent grew within Ordinary, and so did his desire to share his Big Dream. Finally, in despair, he told his Big Dream to his father.

"I'm not surprised," his father responded. "You've had that dream since you were little."

Tears filled Ordinary's eyes. *I was born to fulfill this dream*, he realized.

Then Ordinary's father told him about his own tragic experience. He, too, had been given a Big Dream by the Dream Giver a long, long time ago. He had waited for the right time and the right circumstances to pursue his dream—but the timing was never right, and the circumstances never changed. Soon it was too late, and his dream turned to dust. He had missed his destiny.

"Don't make the same mistake I did, Son," he told Ordinary. "You don't have to be a nobody. You can be a Somebody!"

From that moment on Ordinary decided not to repeat his father's mistake. Over time he made hard choices and difficult changes. Despite pleas from his best friend to stay in the Land of the Familiar, Ordinary left for the Land of the Possibility, humming a tune he'd never heard before. He soon discovered that there were bullies to battle in the Land of the Possibility— discouragement, pessimism, and doubt—but they didn't deter him. He never returned to his old home. Ever. He knew he was born to do more than the ordinary, the comfortable, and the familiar. He was made for a mission.[4]

Are You Pursuing Your Dream?

Now let me meddle in your life for a moment and ask you a personal question: Have you left the Land of the Familiar and visited the Land of the Possibility? Better yet, have you taken up residence?

What about your kids? Have you encouraged them to explore the landscape beyond the city gates? Have you discovered that they were made for a mission? Do you know that the Dream Giver wants to transform each of your kids from an Ordinary to a Somebody?

He does.

Jesus said, "I came that they might have life and might have it abundantly" (John 10:10). That's not to say there won't be challenges to overcome and bullies to overpower. But God has a plan for your life and the lives of each of your kids. He wants you and your kids to be driven by dreams rather than by difficulties. He's a Big God who gives Big Dreams—just as a nobody called Ordinary discovered.

Now here's an important truth I don't want you to miss. Maybe you just read these last few paragraphs, but you still see yourself sitting on the sidelines, wondering if the Dream Giver has a dream for you. It seems as though every other nobody called Ordinary is on the inside, pursuing their dreams, but you're on the outside with your nose pressed against the glass. Well, let me invite you to look again. Not at them, but at yourself. Look deep into your heart. Now do you see it?

The Dream Giver has given every Ordinary a dream.
Only some will embrace it.
Even fewer will pursue it.

There it is, in a box in a corner of a forgotten closet. Dust covers the box; fear covers your spirit. Fearfully you remove the top and look inside. Your eyes fall on something that looks familiar . . . but it's been a long time since you last saw it. It used to be your compass, but then:

- A parent ignored you

- A friend mocked you

- A boyfriend dropped you

- A spouse minimized you

- A coworker criticized you

- A boss fired you

That's when the dream was tucked in a shoebox and stored away.

Now, whenever your kids share their dreams, your response is, "That's nice. Finish your homework." It was difficult to experience the death of your own dream; it would be devastating to watch the demise of theirs. They long to visit the Land of the Possibility, but the roots of the Familiar run deep. *Maybe next year they can branch out*, you think. *Maybe next year the timing will be right and the circumstances will be different.* They won't be, you know . . .

A Dream Come True

Thank God that's not what Wilma's mother thought.

Wilma was born to a poor family in a shack in the backwoods of Tennessee. Premature and weighing only 4.5 pounds, she was the twentieth of twenty-two children. Many people doubted she would survive—but not her mother. During her childhood she was hampered by measles, mumps, and chicken pox. When she was four years old, she had double pneumonia and scarlet fever—then she contracted polio, which resulted in her left leg being paralyzed. Still her mom didn't give up on her. Twice a week for two years, she took Wilma to Meharry Hospital in Nashville, fifty miles away, until Wilma could walk with a brace.

Wilma's mother knew her daughter may be weak, but she wasn't worthless. In fact, Wilma's mother taught all twenty-two of her children to dream bigger than their circumstances. No exception was made for a kid in a leg brace. This brave mother helped her daughter develop an invincible spirit—the key that would carry her to the highest podium in the world.

At nine years of age Wilma removed her leg brace and took the step that her doctors had told her was medically impossible.

By the time she was thirteen, she was able to trot. Her doctors called it a miracle. In junior high Wilma turned her trot into a gallop and followed her older sister Yolanda onto the basketball court. The coach didn't put her into a single game—for three years.

At thirteen Wilma decided to try track, and she entered her first race. She came in last—dead last. That didn't dent her dream, however. She entered every race she could and consistently finished last in them all. Her friends begged her to quit, but her mother encouraged her to continue. "Dreams need demonstration," her mother said.

Then one day Wilma experienced a miracle. She ran a race and didn't finish last. She came in next to last. Not long after that she ran a race and actually won. As a result she caught the attention of her high-school basketball coach, who asked her to join the team her sophomore year. From then on Wilma Rudolph won every race she ran throughout the remainder of high school.

Some time later Ed Temple, the women's track coach for Tennessee State University, saw Wilma play basketball. He couldn't help but notice the nimble, fleet-footed guard. Coach Temple not only noticed Wilma's skills; more importantly, he noticed her spirit. That's what told him she would be a winner.

> Those who say that good things come in small packages
> are usually talking about diamonds in a box.
> Wilma was a diamond in the rough.

When Wilma received a full scholarship to attend Tennessee State University, Coach Temple had his hands full. Wilma's spirit was resolute, but her talent was raw. Both pupil and professor worked hard, and finally their dreams became reality.

In the 1956 Olympic Games in Melbourne, Australia, Wilma won a bronze medal for the United States in the 400 meter relay race.

The third-place finish turned out to be just an Olympic appetizer.

At the 1960 Olympic Games in Rome, Wilma was pitted against the fastest woman of her day, Jutta Heine of Germany. Even though Jutta had never lost a race, Wilma was undaunted. She had learned something from her challenging childhood: dream big and do your best.

Over the next few days Wilma Rudolph accomplished the inconceivable. She beat Jutta in the 100 meter dash. She beat Jutta again in the 200 meter dash. Finally, in the 400 meter relay Wilma was matched against Jutta once more. Both were running the "anchor" leg for their teams. Through three-quarters of the race, the Germans and Americans were neck and neck. Then the third American runner reached out to pass the baton to Wilma—and dropped it in her excitement. Jutta dashed away. Wilma's dream seemed to do the same.

> But big dreams don't die easily—
> especially when they've been forged by fire.

Wilma picked up the baton and started running with everything she had in her. She quickly regained lost ground and accomplished the impossible: she beat Jutta again and won the race for the Americans. Three Olympic races, three Olympic gold medals—three Olympic-sized dreams fulfilled.[5]

Diamonds, Dollars, and Dreams

Remember when you were young and your mother wanted to make a point but didn't have the time? She'd say things like:

"Read between the lines," "Look before you leap," and "Money doesn't grow on trees." My mom said them, I remembered them, and now I repeat them to my kids.

"All good things come in small packages" falls into the same category. Most of us probably heard it from our parents. We've probably said it to our kids. But what can we really conclude about it? Well, if you're talking about diamonds or dollars, you're right; good things do come in small packages. If you're talking about pint-size soccer players with plus-size dreams like Sara Webster's, you're right again. If you're talking about cars, computers, or cell phones, "small" is definitely the new "big."

But if you're talking about dreams, bigger is definitely better.

In previous chapters I stated that our kids need to dream with their eyes open and their feet on the ground. This minimizes "delusional dreams." I also mentioned that kids need to progress from dreaming to doing with purpose and perseverance in order to make their dreams come true. This minimizes "dormant dreams." We also need to encourage our children to *dream big*—because this minimizes "deficient dreams."

How can we do this? Here are some suggestions:

1. *Teach your kids the significance of "dreaming," as well as the importance of "doing."* We live in an age where there's an abundance of doers and a shortage of dreamers. Encourage your kids to dream—and dream BIG. But never undervalue the importance of "doing." Dreamers believe it will happen, doers will make it happen . . . and spectators will watch it happen. Teach your kids to dream it—then do it.

2. *Give your young dreamer telescopes rather than microscopes.* Encourage your kids to reach for the stars and not get sidetracked by the specifics. Tell them stories of ordinary people who achieved extraordinary accomplishments because they were driven by their dreams. Dreaming bigger than their abilities gives God a chance to show up and take their dreams from good to great.

3. *Model the process of dreaming big for your kids.* Let them know about your own big dreams by sharing with them what's on your mind and on your prayer list.

4. *Help your kids define their dreams by talking about them.* Write their dreams on note cards, and stick them on their bedroom mirror or the refrigerator door. When we voice them, print them, and post them, it's easier to look back and see how the Dream Giver helped us accomplish them.

5. *Pray for your kids' dreams when you tuck them in bed at night.* Bedtime is a great time to let them know who the Dream Giver really is.

Who knows? Underneath your nose may sit the next soccer superstar or Olympic gold medalist. Why dream average? Personally, I think that "average" is highly overrated.

19

THE LIE

The Best Things in Life Are Free

THE BEST THINGS IN LIFE MAY BE FREE,
BUT SOMEONE STILL HAS TO PAY SHIPPING AND HANDLING.

Ryan heard it at home, he heard it at school, and he heard it at church. Given the right situation and the right application, it was true. Unfortunately, when it was applied outside those examples . . . this premise had a problem.

"The best things in life are free."
Really?

As a toddler Ryan had been to McDonald's a million times. There he experienced the saying, even before he heard it. McDonald's is just one of a dozen fast-food restaurants that believe in the benefits of "free" to attract a customer: "Buy a Happy Meal, get a free toy." At first the "McTrinket" got more of Ryan's attention than the McNuggets. Free was fantastic! But before long his fascination with the free grew faint. To Ryan the free toy became as valuable as a tricycle to a teenager. Soon the trinket found its way to the back-seat floor. Valueless.

When Ryan was seven, he made his plea to visit Mickey,

Minnie, and Donald. That's when he first actually heard the phrase "The best things in life are free"—as his mom took him by the hand to the park down the street. He had envisioned Disneyland. Instead, he got "Playland." It was free, but not fantastic.

Over the years that followed, Ryan continually heard this premise playing in the background of his life: on commercials highlighting sunset walks on the beach, at the supper table when times were tough, and at church emphasizing a life dedicated to the Divine. In those situations, "the best things in life are free" rang true. But the premise clearly was not absolute.

One Christmas morning thirteen-year-old Ryan unwrapped his new electric guitar with excitement and anticipation. It cost his parents $215 to buy it—it cost Ryan nothing to unwrap it. At first the guitar was played regularly. Soon regularly became rarely, and rarely became never. Now the guitar sits in the corner of the closet, two strings missing, collecting dust. Valueless.

At seventeen Ryan was given a free T-shirt at a concert. At first he wore it on school days to advertise his attendance at the concert to his peers. After a few months he only wore it on Saturdays when he cleaned his car. Later he *used* it on Saturdays to clean his car. You can predict its final resting spot. It's well on the way to being valueless.

No wonder Ryan is confused. He heard the premise from his parents, when they used it to emphasize the value of the priceless. Unfortunately, over time, he translated it to minimize the value of the costless. If Ryan's parents don't explain the difference to him, he's likely to apply this myth—"the best things in life are free"—to the value of a relationship . . . and that may cost him here on earth, as well as in the life to come.

Free-for-All

Some people say, "The best things in life are free." Others say, "Money makes the world go around." Still others tell us, "There's no such thing as a free lunch." Confused? I know this: when people tell me they know how to get something significant for free, I look for signs of a concussion. The only thing in life that's free is advice . . . and you usually get what you pay for.

From what I understand, the best things in life *used* to be free. Of course, that was back in the Garden of Eden. Since then the price has gone up. It now includes shipping and handling.

When I was a kid, I used to go swimming at the YMCA. It was free. I'd swim for an hour, play basketball for an hour, and lift weights for an hour. I came home bushed and buffed. Now, even the Y costs $400 a year. If you prefer a "designer" workout on equipment like the Ironman 320e Elliptical in front of wall-to-wall mirrors and flat-screen TVs, you can join a fitness center for a one-time fee of $195 plus $65 a month.

**When fitness became high fashion,
fitness became high priced.**

Did you ever think you'd see the day when you'd pay a buck for a bottle of water? It contains no caffeine, no calories, and no sugar. I think the buck is for the bottle! For the money you pay, you'd think Ozarka Natural Spring Water was extracted from an artesian well hidden deep within the Ozark Mountains. It isn't. It's bottled in Texas. By the way, if it *were* drawn from mineral-rich water pockets located miles beneath the surface of the earth, it would be warm, not wintry.

It seems to me that if my dog can lap water from a puddle

or quench his thirst from the toilet and live to be eighty-six in dog years, then tap water is good enough for me. Soon we'll be lining up for bottled air! Well, actually . . . we are. An oxygen-rich bottle of Blue Air costs $24.95 and is good for fifty to seventy-five breaths. It's selling like hot cakes.

While manufacturers have put price tags on air and water, marketers have discovered that in America, "free" sells. We live in a country that was built on "free"—free will, free speech, free trade. This is the land of the free. From the simple to the significant, if it's free, we'll take it!

If you have access to the Internet site www.totallyfreestuff .com, you've just found the mother lode of "free." Whether you want diapers or digital cameras, sunglasses or cell phones, you just pick your product, place your order, and start checking your mail box. It's free. No effort, no charge, no sweat. (Well, you do have to fill out a questionnaire or two, but that shouldn't take you more than a week.)

On a Saturday morning drive there's nothing like a cool morning breeze, a fresh cup of coffee—and a "free" car wash. Decorated telephone poles and roadside cheerleaders waving billboard-sized posters direct me to pull my car up to the bucket brigade in the parking lot, so they can turn filthy into flawless—for free. (But then, the fine print reads, "Donations accepted.")

Credit-card companies used to flood mailboxes with offers of low introductory rates. That worked for a while. Now they offer "free." Free frequent-flier miles. Free coupons from retailers like the Gap. Chase recently offered the free StockBack MasterCard: for every $100 you charge, they'll put one dollar into a brokerage account for you to invest or take as cash. Most banks have followed suit with offers for free checks, free ATM machines, and free online banking. (Of course, it's all free as long as you use their card or put your money in their bank.)

In just forty years America has gone from "free sex" to "free stuff." I love this country.

But turn the corner with me now from the material to the more meaningful: the warmth of a candlelight dinner, the smell of a newborn baby, the splendor of a spring day. These free delights fall under the category of "things that really matter." They go beyond the material to enrich the soul and encourage the spirit. They're free to those who desire richness of life rather than just richness of luxury.

The list is endless:

- The sound of your child's prayers at night

- The scent in the air after an evening thunderstorm

- The love that swells just before you say, "I do"

- The accomplishment you feel when you graduate from college

- The warmth of your dad's wink after you introduce him to your date

- The joy you feel with your child's every accomplishment

- The colors you see at sunset as the sun kisses the Pacific Ocean

- The relief that comes from finding the hamster that's been lost in the house for a week!

Holding the delicate hand of your toddler provides significance; holding the calloused hand of your husband provides security. Both are priceless . . . and both are free.

> But "free" isn't always as free as it seems.
> Sometimes "free" can be costly.

When the Valuable Becomes Valueless

Countering the "best things in life are free" premise is another premise: "You value what you pay for." At McDonald's, Ryan pays nothing for a trinket; soon it becomes valueless. "That's OK; there'll be another one to replace it tomorrow." For Christmas, Ryan pays nothing for a guitar; soon it becomes valueless. "That's OK; easy come, easy go." As a teenager, Ryan pays nothing for a T-shirt; soon it's a castoff destined to be a car rag. "That's OK; there are more where that one came from."

When a toddler is told that a particular toy will be his only toy, however, watch how it's treated. When a thirteen-year-old purchases a guitar with his own lawn-cutting money, watch how it's cared for. When a teenager pays full price for a shirt, watch how it's cared for—more like cashmere than cotton.

There's a related and revealing principle that says this: not only do you value what you pay for, but you value it to the degree that *you* pay for it. Full price equals full value. Discounted price equals discounted value. Try it yourself: Pay $19.95 for a blouse off the sale rack and see how you treat it. Pay $99 for a blouse off the designer rack and see how you treat *it*.

The things that count the most
are the things that cost the most.

Nowhere is this truer than when it comes to relationships.

TRUTH OR CONSEQUENCES

Some say that love is free. They're wrong. Forty years ago, what was called "free love" was actually "free sex." Sex can be free—but love never has been, never will be. The fact that love costs is the reason that love has value. Love pays a voluntary cost, but a necessary one. Loving partners and loving parents voluntarily give, voluntarily sacrifice, and voluntarily forfeit personal pleasures to ensure the well-being of those they love. They work extra jobs in order to provide extra pleasures. They shower up, show up (and sometimes shut up) in order to respect and honor a loved one.

THE TRUTH

Some things in life are free, but most things are valued proportionate to their cost—especially relationships.

This truth opens the door to a number of issues that our kids need to understand . . . but won't find covered in any high-school curriculum. Applying the concept of "value" to the *relational* as well as the *tangible* is critical to unraveling the deception behind the blanket acceptance of the message, "The best things in life are free."

Here are a few points about the value of relationships to share with your kids:

1. *People value what they pay for, and they value it in proportion to what it costs them.* This is as true of relationships as it is of material possessions.

2. *"Cost free" relationships are devalued and lose their worth over time,* while "costly" relationships are valued and gain in worth over time.

3. *Commitment and fidelity hold a marriage together.* Neither is cost free. Eliminate these qualities from a marriage, and you eliminate the value of the marriage.

4. *If you "discount" a relationship by lowering your standards or reducing your expectations, you devalue the relationship and reduce its worth.* If you "discount" your values, your standards, or your boundaries by 25 percent in order to be with someone "special," you discount the value of your relationship by the same percentage. (Ever wonder why someone doesn't respect you? Maybe they got the message that you discounted yourself to be with them, and they devalued you just as they would an item from the sale rack.)

Whether with our companions, our kids, or our colleagues, we invest time, money, and effort in our relationships, and because of that, they have value. The more we invest, the more valuable these relationships become. High-priced relationships are high-value relationships. That's why, after a nine-month pregnancy followed by twelve months of sleep deprivation and 6,000 dirty-diaper changes, a mother could wrestle a grizzly to the ground if her child were in jeopardy.

Motivated by Love

A story is told of two warring tribes in the Andes—one that lived in the valley and one that lived in the mountains high above. One day the mountain tribe invaded the lowland tribe, and as part of their plunder, they kidnapped a baby and brought it back to their mountain village.

Even though the people in the valley didn't know how to climb the treacherous rock cliffs that separated the two tribes, they sent their best warriors to rescue the baby and return it to its family. The warriors tried one method to scale the cliffs, then another, then another. Finally, after several days they realized the cause was hopeless. They had climbed only a few hundred feet, and many of their warriors had already fallen to their deaths.

As they prepared to return to their village in the valley, they looked up and saw a woman walking down from the mountain toward them, holding a baby in her arms. It was the baby they had tried to rescue being carried by its mother.

"We couldn't climb that mountain, even with our strongest warriors!" the leader of the rescue team exclaimed. "How did you climb these cliffs and rescue the child?"

The mother shrugged and said, "It wasn't your baby."[1]

Bought and Paid For

Relationships aren't free. But there is one that's been bought and paid for by Someone else. Christ sacrificed his life to give us abundant life here on earth and eternal life when we leave. He paid the price because he knew we couldn't afford the payments.

Ryan may miss this offer, thinking there's no such thing as

a free lunch. He's partly right. With God you don't get a free lunch; you get breakfast and dinner too.

Tell your kids the truth: we value what we pay for, but money can't buy the most important things in life.

The best things in this life aren't free—
but the best things in the life to come are. Kids like Ryan are counting on us to tell them the difference.

THE LIE

If It Doesn't Kill You, It Will Make You Stronger

ONE LEARNS MORE FROM TEN DAYS OF AGONY
THAN FROM TEN YEARS OF CONTENTMENT.

Merle Shain

You know this type of story—maybe all too well. During a two-year span of adversity, a family's life would plunge from tranquil to tragic. The transformation would be almost inconceivable.

For Todd and Peggy Schilling, life was bliss. Money was plentiful, jobs were purposeful, and marriage was meaningful. Peggy described Todd as blameless and baby-faced. Their relationship was a fairy-tale romance laced with flowers and favors. But Todd and Peggy were about to be forged by fire. The blacksmith was at their doorstep, and the heat of the hearth was going to singe their hearts.

While pregnant with their second child, Peggy was hit by a drunk driver. Her neck was broken in three places. After visiting Peggy in the hospital, Todd left the parking garage on his motorcycle and was hit on the head by a metal gate that descended from the ceiling. The gate crushed Todd's spine, leaving him with a fractured neck in two places, a fractured lower back in three places, two broken wrists, and a broken jaw.

During Peggy's surgery, an anesthesiologist intubated her incorrectly, leaving her with a damaged left vocal chord. Peggy would speak faintly for the rest of her life. The pleasure she enjoyed from singing at church would be permanently suspended.

These would be minor inconveniences compared to what was around the corner. Two months later, Todd and Peggy stood side by side in a neonatal hospital room and said goodbye to their newborn son.

The calamity continued.

Todd developed a rare eye disease called *keratoconus*, which required a cornea transplant in his left eye. Following the surgery, he flew to Montana to attend his grandfather's funeral. After the funeral, signs of cornea rejection appeared, and Todd returned to the hospital for emergency surgery. The next day he was told the doctor had implanted an infected cornea. As a result Todd would have to receive injections in his left eye every other day for the next two months to try to save his sight.

The hardship persisted.

While at the hospital, Todd and Peggy's home was ransacked. Their hearts were ravaged. Everything of value was gone. Not even their home could protect them from the relentless adversity that followed them like a starving lion stalking its prey.

Todd underwent surgery to repair the damage that had been done to his lower back. Neurosurgeons braced his spine with bolts and brackets. It was the best they could do. Unfortunately, it couldn't protect him from a neurological disorder that has a history of reducing the bravest warrior to rubble. Shortly after his surgery Todd was diagnosed with Reflex Sympathetic Dystrophy. This nervous-system disorder, first identified during the Civil War, is relatively rare, but it's both physically debilitating and psychologically devastating. Symptoms include severe chronic muscle pain, changes in skin color, hypersensitivity to touch, and swelling. In Todd's case it began to destroy the nerves and blood vessels in his feet. Then it slowly inched upward. His legs turned blue. His future turned bleak. Morphine made the pain tolerable—but his prognosis was anything but favorable.

The final blow was delivered by Todd's doctor. His recommendation was amputation. It was Todd's only hope. It would save his life but not end his pain.

Todd was on the anvil.
The blacksmith's hammer was brutal.
Todd was crushed—but not conquered.

Given the situation, Todd's response was surprising. "There's no way I can make that choice," he said. "I just can't do it. I don't know what you believe, Doctor, but I believe that God can heal me."

Given the situation, the doctor's answer was sobering: "I sure hope so, Todd, because that's the only hope you've got. If you are going to do anything with your family, do it now, and we'll discuss this more on your next visit."

Doctor-patient information is confidential. Neither said anything to Peggy. She was pregnant again. Instead, Todd suggested that he and Peggy get away to Florida to see her parents. Despite his faith, his body was telling him this could be his last trip. Peggy didn't need to know.

I know what you're thinking. You're waiting for me to turn the corner and get to the silver lining, the happy ending.

You'll have to wait. What came next would test the character of Joseph, the courage of David, and the faith of Job. I cringe when I say this, but things only got worse.

The day Todd and Peggy arrived in Florida, the engine blew up in their rental car. Two days later, when they were returning from the beach, a fully-loaded semitruck plowed into the back of their car at a four-way stop. Peggy went into premature labor. Todd's jaw and both wrists were broken—again.

What they needed from their friends was support. What they heard from their friends was sarcasm:

> "Don't get in a car with Todd and Peggy;
> you'll never get out alive."
> "Don't walk too close to Todd and Peggy;
> lightening might strike."

Todd and Peggy were at the end of their rope. The flames of the blacksmith had melted their joy. The hammer of the blacksmith had crushed their will. The anvil of the blacksmith had shattered their spirits. Many have been leveled by less. Would Todd and Peggy be defeated—or developed?[1]

More later.

Circumstances That Warrant an Explanation

No parent can explain to a toddler the benefits of cancer— the personal development that comes with chemotherapy. No parent can rationalize years of sexual abuse to a teenager by pointing to personal growth as a plus. No parent can convince a child of the fringe benefits of discrimination or the long-term profit of prejudice. Each of these calamities will leave scars that will remain long after the words are spoken: "If it doesn't kill you, it will make you stronger." In an attempt to rationalize the unexplainable to our kids, we grope for words that offer understanding. We end up giving pat answers and platitudes that contain a ring of truth but a centerpiece of fallacy:

- Marcy was born with a birth defect. Her skin is discolored, and multiple noncancerous tumors have developed throughout her nerves and skin. It's called Recklinghausen's Disease. Her parents tell her that God made her "special" and that someday she will be thankful.

- Dillon was eight when it began. At first he was pushed, then he was slapped. Now he's ten, and his two years of physical abuse have resulted in beatings, bruises, and two broken bones. When his stepfather was finally arrested, he shouted to Dillon, "I only did it to make you stronger!"

- Marcus is too young to understand why his dad lost his job as pastor of the church, but he isn't too young to experience the impact. Tension fills the air; fear fills his heart. Within weeks his dad has gone from being the pastor to being a painter. At school he notices the whispers but seldom hears the words. What he does hear smacks of satire and sarcasm. At home, when tears fill his eyes, his mom tries to comfort his heart: "It's OK. We'll get over this, and when we do, we'll be stronger for it."

It's the "strength by strain" theory, and it's partly true. There *are* payoffs to pain, but not all the time, and not in all circumstances. Unfortunately, that part of the message is not always communicated.

The sentiment, "That which doesn't kill makes you stronger," was birthed from the pen of the nineteenth-century German philosopher Friedrich Nietzsche. His life both confirmed and contradicted the words he wrote. When his father, a Lutheran pastor, died, four-year-old Friedrich responded with great drive and determination. Later in life, when Nietzsche contracted diphtheria and dysentery, he pressed on. Despite several romantic setbacks, his most productive years followed these misfortunes.

Gaining insight from each blow, Nietzsche could have worn the crown of "Crushed but Not Conquered"—until the morning of January 3, 1889. While in Turin, Italy, Nietzsche was devastated when he witnessed a horse being beaten by its owner. He threw his arms around the wounded animal and collapsed from a nervous breakdown. Nietzsche was labeled "insane" and never returned to writing. He had to be cared for by his sister Elizabeth until he died eleven years later.[2]

Despite that final turn of events, recent studies show that perhaps Nietzsche was right after all: character is developed more by trial than by triumph. In 1962 a landmark research project was conducted, and the results were published in a journal article titled "Cradles of Eminence." The study, directed by husband-and-wife team Victor and Mildred Goertzel, focused on the lives of 413 famous and exceptionally accomplished individuals. The Goertzels spent years looking for the one common denominator that might account for the success of this group. Finally, they found it.

After examining a number of variables, they discovered that 392 out of the 413 individuals in the study—95 percent—had overcome extremely difficult personal or family circumstances.

One single factor stood at the center of all their accomplishments: perseverance. They had been battered but not broken. Tempered by life's grueling circumstances, they had become strong, stable, and resistant to setbacks.[3]

Strengthened by Our Circumstances

In 1984 Robert Schuller published a book titled *Tough Times Never Last, but Tough People Do!* More than one million copies were sold; the book spent more than three months on the *New York Times* bestseller list. The message of the manuscript was clear: what lies behind us and what lies before us are insignificant when compared to what lies within us.[4] Especially if what lies within us has been strengthened by circumstances . . .

In September 2005, four-time Grammy-award winner Olivia Newton-John was on the cover of *Parade* magazine under the headline "Stronger Than Before." That's also the title of her newest album, which features a number of artists who are breast-cancer survivors like herself.[5]

A kite soars against the wind, not with it.

Quadriplegic author, artist, and popular speaker Joni Eareckson Tada has been confined to a wheelchair since a tragic diving accident as a teenager in 1967. Rather than live a life of resignation, Joni has authored thirty books, spoken in more than thirty-five countries, and served on the National Council on Disability when the Americans with Disabilities Act became law. When asked what she might say to God about her disability when she arrives in heaven, Joni said her first words would be, "Thanks, I needed that!"[6]

Muscles are built by strain, not sloth.

Most people know about Erin Brockovich because of the performance of Academy Award–winning actress Julia Roberts, who played Erin in the movie bearing her name. Erin was the inexperienced but tenacious law secretary who fought for the 630 residents of Hinkley, California, in a suit against the Pacific Gas and Electric Company. What most don't know, however, is that Erin attributed her success to two adversities: dyslexia and desperation. According to Brockovich, her dyslexia led to her being labeled "retarded" as a child, forcing her to develop her instinctual skills over her intellectual skills. Ultimately her keen instincts were what convinced her that the residents of Hinkley weren't lying about the impact of PG&E's water contamination on their community's health.

Erin was also desperate. She had two failed marriages under her belt, three small children at her feet, cramped quarters, bare cupboards, a depleted bank account, and a herniated disc from a recent car accident. When her lawsuit against the driver of the car that hit her was dismissed, she knew she had reached the end of her rope. She begged her lawyer, Ed Masry, to hire her as his secretary. He did, and the rest is history. Together they took on PG&E, and in 1996 they won a settlement of $333 million—the largest settlement in a direct-action lawsuit in U.S. history.[7]

Tough times strengthen character the same way a vaccination strengthens the immune system. Measles, mumps, rubella, polio, chickenpox, and tetanus are all prevented by first introducing a small amount of disease-causing germs into our bodies. The germs strengthen our immune systems, enabling us to overpower more deadly viral concentrations if we're exposed in the future. Other studies have confirmed the benefits of strength by strain time and time again:

- For many years the prevailing theory of radiation risk suggested that any increase in radiation exposure would increase the risk of cancer. Actually, research by biologist Ronald Mitchel suggests just the opposite. He determined that while high doses of radiation do increase the likelihood of cancer (as expected), a low dosage of radiation actually stimulates DNA repair, delaying the onset of cancer in mice.[8]

- While prolonged exposure to extreme temperatures is harmful to skin cells, physiologist Suresh Rattan discovered that heating the skin to about 100 degrees Fahrenheit twice a week for about an hour each time actually increases skin health by slowing the aging of skin cells.[9]

- The definitive study by Richard Kociba in 1978 linking high doses of dioxin to high rates of cancer in rats also determined that low doses of dioxin actually reduce the prevalence of tumors in rats.[10]

TRUTH OR CONSEQUENCES

Allow me to summarize our situation by defining our dilemma:

Is character developed by adversity? Definitely.
Is faith deepened during hardship? Absolutely.
Is perseverance strengthened by strain? Unquestionably.
Should we be giddy when tough times come? Not a chance!

This understanding must first be digested by parents before it can be described to kids. In an attempt to explain tough times, we often look for a rationale that will bring hope to a broken heart or clarity to a dire circumstance. While the cliché "If it doesn't kill you, it will make you stronger" may explain the fact that there are payoffs to pain, it also suggests that we should welcome whatever hurts. Like cod liver oil, it's good for you. Take it like a man. You'll get over it. Keep a stiff upper lip.

The truth is that the brokenhearted benefit more from compassion than from conclusions. The difference between those who offer compassion and those who offer a cliché for every calamity is like the difference between a surgeon and a mechanic. Both are well-intentioned. Both are good with the tools of their trade. Only one can heal a broken heart.

Just ask Todd and Peggy.

The semitruck accident in Florida had taken its toll; it was the last straw. Todd and Peggy could take no more. Doctors suggested that they return home as soon as possible. Sent packing like lepers, they were physically disabled, emotionally drained, and spiritually depleted.

Todd was the first to fall down but look up. "Whatever you are trying to teach me, I promise I'll learn," he prayed. "Why do we have to keep going through these things? I promise you—I'll learn, I'll learn!"

Then came Peggy. For her, like Todd, the burden had become unbearable. From behind the door of the hotel bathroom, she cried out to God. She hung her head and sobbed uncontrollably. Then her breakthrough came—she sensed God asking her to praise him.

He'd heard her cry.
He knew her pain.
He had seen her before.

Peggy was the woman in the crowd who had been bleeding for twelve years—the one who reached out to touch the hem of his robe.[11] Her burden was too much to bear. She couldn't muster the courage to come face to face with him, but she believed that if she could just get close enough, he would heal her.

Peggy couldn't get close enough to touch the hem of his robe, but she could praise her way into his presence.

**Praise unlocks the door to healing,
because it connects the hurting to the Healer.**

Peggy began to praise God. "Praise the Lord. Praise the Lord," she cried.

Her words opened her heart. Her Healer opened his hands. And his presence opened her eyes—he had been there all the time.

Peggy's father suggested that before she and Todd left Florida, the couple should attend a special church service that was taking place in town. They arrived early in order to get seats with others like themselves: the afflicted, the ailing, and the outcast.

While waiting for the service to begin, an elderly woman spotted Todd. "Sweetheart," she said, "I don't know what your need is, but God told me that he is going to heal you." She prayed a simple prayer and then made a stunning request: "Get up." Striving beyond his circumstances, Todd tried to escape the confines of his wheelchair. His first step was agonizing. His second step wasn't much better. Then . . . it happened. With his third step he set foot in a new land—the land of the liberated, the home of the healed. Todd took off running and didn't stop until he had circled the arena three times. Victory laps.

To this day Todd is symptom free. His doctor recorded his

recovery as a medical miracle. And Peggy? She's the proud mother of a healthy baby girl named Ashley.[12]

So what's the truth we need to tell our kids? Simply this:

THE TRUTH

Character is developed more by strain than by success. But strength comes from the Savior and is found most often by those on their knees.

The Bible puts it this way in Isaiah 40:31 (KJV):

> But they that wait upon the LORD shall renew their
>   strength;
> they shall mount up with wings like eagles;
>   they shall run, and not be weary;
>   and they shall walk, and not faint.

The hardship and heartache Todd and Peggy suffered didn't kill them, but it didn't make them stronger either. It made them weak . . . and drove them to their knees. That's where they found a miracle and a Master—one for this life and for the life to come.

21

THE LIE
Silence Is Golden

PARENTS ARE THE LAST PEOPLE ON EARTH
WHO OUGHT TO HAVE CHILDREN.

Samuel Butler

In a world filled with endless uncertainty, most people want to know what they can count on these days. Unfortunately, the list is short.

Not long ago I challenged a group of moms to name a few things they knew they could count on. They told me that after death and taxes, the list got really bleak! When pressed a little further, they explained:

- If you send your husband to the store to pick up three items and then add one more as an afterthought, you can count on his picking up the last item you mentioned and forgetting the first three.

- If you planned on eating the candy bar on the way home from the grocery store, you can count on it being hidden somewhere at the bottom of the heaviest bag.

- If your insurance policy states it will cover all damages incurred to your vehicle following an accident, you can count on it covering all damages incurred to your car except the damage caused by the accident.

- If you leave work two hours late because you decided to stay and finish a task, you can be sure it will go unnoticed. If you leave work ten minutes early to get the kids to the dentist, you can count on running into the boss in the parking lot.

- If you choose the shortest checkout line at the grocery store, you can be sure the person in front of you will need a price check on aisle 13.

- When you finally receive the pay raise your boss promised you two years ago, you can be sure it will be just enough to increase your tax bracket but decrease your take-home pay.

Isn't that encouraging?

Adults aren't the only ones who want to know what they can count on—our kids wonder the same thing. From toddlers to teenagers, most kids live in a world that seems even more uncertain to them than our world does to us. This leaves them even more desperate to find something to anchor their unsteady lives to. For most kids, parents are the natural choice.

However, for the past twenty chapters we've tossed up the notion that while most of us are well-intentioned, we've fed our kids a diet of clichés that have contained a little bit of fact . . . and a little bit of fiction. We ourselves heard the lies. We remembered the lies. We repeated the lies.

> Our kids have counted on us to tell them the truth,
> the whole truth, and nothing but the truth.
> Unfortunately, we've had to plead the Fifth a few times.

That's OK. We're not perfect—we're parents. From this day forward we will take the oath to separate fact from fiction. Now that we know better, we will do better—for our kids' sakes.

Now turn the corner with me. There's one last lie we promote by our silence rather than our speech. Our silence is shouting a message to our kids that we may not intend, but a message they hear loud and clear.

When Silence Isn't Golden

Let me introduce you to Michelle, Josh, and Eric. They are all fourteen. Besides age, they have another glaring similarity: each of them lives in a home where silence is anything but golden.

Michelle . . .

Michelle came home from school today, just like she has every school day for the past nine years. Unfortunately, today wasn't like any other day. In health class Michelle was told how to open the small rubber package, carefully remove its contents . . . and then roll the condom down over the banana, simulating what she or her boyfriend would do before they have sex. This would make their sex "safe" and eliminate any of the consequences she might otherwise experience from premarital intercourse.

"Be prepared," she was told. "After all, everybody's doing it"—so this is what she needed to do to protect herself from an unwanted pregnancy or sexually transmitted disease.

Michelle was horrified by the demonstration but said

nothing during class. She simply followed the instructions and did her best to camouflage her anxiety and conceal her embarrassment.

At the dinner table that night, Michelle's mom asked, "How was school today?"

"Um, fine, I guess." Michelle wanted to talk about what happened in class, but she was paralyzed by her parents' prohibition: They never talked about sex. It was forbidden territory. While Mom and Michelle had "the talk" when she was twelve, it was hard to tell who was more uneasy during the nineteen-minute conversation—mother or daughter. That was the last time the word *sex* was spoken.

Besides being fearful to venture into this classified content, Michelle was fearful of how her parents might react. What if they phoned the school and confronted her teacher? She would be humiliated! From that moment on she would be tagged by her teacher and seared by her schoolmates. She would be labeled out-of-touch, out-to-lunch, and out-of-circulation.

So she said nothing. Her parents noticed she was particularly quiet at the dinner table, but they said nothing too. Silence on this subject filled the supper conversation.

Josh . . .

Josh is a typical teenager. He's in the ninth grade at Cedar Valley High. His priorities are playing sports, watching sports, and reading about sports—in that order. Grades are a distant fourth. Real distant.

Last Friday night Josh went over to Rob's house to hang out. No big deal. At about seven, Rob's parents decided to go to the movies. No big deal. They would only be gone a few hours. They would have their cell phone, so if there were any problems, Rob was to call.

By 7:30 Rob and Josh were bored and looking for buddies. Messages were sent by every communication device known to mankind except smoke signals: text messages, phone calls, IMs, and e-mails. The word got out. Friends showed up. The kids stayed outside on the porch. No problems so far.

Then things changed. Fifteen-year-old Justin came to Rob's house with more than "hanging out" in mind. You could smell it on his breath. Partially wasted from drinking, he quickly became the life of the party. The two bottles of alcohol he took from his parents' bar wouldn't be missed, and he was willing to share with everyone. For those who really wanted to take a ride on the wild side, he also had a few ecstasy pills he stole from his older brother's stash. Justin was a traveling drug store. He came equipped.

To make a long story short—some did and some didn't. In case you're wondering, Rob did; Josh didn't. Everyone left Rob's house before his parents returned home, and Mom and Dad were none the wiser. The furniture was in place, Rob was in his room, and Josh was on his way home.

When Josh arrived home at ten, his parents were in the family room watching the news. Josh sat down on the sofa. There was plenty on his mind but little on his lips. "Have fun tonight at Rob's?" his mom asked. "Yeah . . . I guess so," Josh said with hesitation. His mom thought about asking for details, but her hesitation was greater than his. She said nothing. "Great," was the last word Josh heard from his dad as the late-night news anchors filled the family room with talk.

His parents went to bed after the weather. Josh went to bed after the sports. Neither said anything more about the night. Silence.

Eric . . .

Eric was described as a smart, sweet-faced, and soft-spoken kid. He was also the proud proprietor of the hottest game going. For just $69.95 he bought a game that promised to deliver more bang for the buck. Literally. Considered to be the most violent video game of its day, DOOM features some of the most realistic and bloodthirsty scenes of maiming and mutilation that have ever been seen on the small screen. By all reports, it's well on the way to becoming the highest-selling video game in the history of the industry.

Eric's parents preached a message of homework and hard work in order to succeed. To escape the pressure, Eric descended into his basement bedroom and ventured deeper and deeper into his fantasy world of video violence. He could identify with the game's slogan: "DOOM—where the sanest place is behind a trigger." He spent hours in front of the screen mowing down the enemy with bullets, bombs, and bayonets. While playing DOOM, he often listened to the German rock group Rammstein, whose lyrics were filled with messages of murder, mayhem, and massacre. His parents wondered why he spent so much time in his bedroom—but they said nothing, asked nothing, did nothing. *Typical teenager*, they figured.

Two years later Eric and his buddy were bored with setting off firecrackers on a Friday night, so they broke into a white van that was parked on the side of the road. They stole a briefcase, electrical equipment, and sunglasses. While they surveyed their spoils in Eric's gray Honda Prelude, a sheriff's deputy stumbled upon the bumbling adolescent bandits. They were cuffed and charged with theft, criminal mischief, and criminal trespassing.

Eric's parents portrayed the event as a simple case of

teenage mischief. Judge John DeVita saw it differently. He sentenced Eric to counseling, community service, and anger-management classes. Eric feigned remorse and was given early release.

Following that event, Eric changed. At school he felt more like a foreigner than a friend. At home he grew more distant and depressed. His parents were unprepared for what was about to come. Despite their parental suspicions, they remained silent.

Michelle, Josh, and Eric each had parents who were silent when they should have been outspoken. Because of their silence, the ways of the world went unchallenged and the struggles within their kids' spirits went overlooked.

Our silence speaks volumes.
And it's not the message our kids need to hear.

The Lies We Ignore

Our silence is deafening. We're fearful of intruding. We wonder if it's just another stage. We hope they'll get over it or grow out of it. We keep our fingers crossed.

We pray; we prod; we punish.

There were times when you stepped in and wished you hadn't. I understand. Trying to make things better, somehow they got worse. The gap widened, the tension grew, and the issue became larger than life. That's when you decided to step back. Believe me, I understand.

But the message of this chapter is this: *back* is not *better*. This is the time to step up, not out. After all, if we don't speak up, then the message of our culture becomes the only one they hear—and that message is filled with three lies we need to confront. Lies we promote by our silence.

Lie #1: Sex Is Safe

For the past fifty years the entertainment industry has been fascinated with sex. Unfortunately, they're not alone. Marketing executives in Manhattan know sex sells. Just ask youth retailer Abercrombie and Fitch.

If you venture into the A&F store at your local mall, be prepared to cover your eyes. Decorating the walls are larger-than-life pictures of kids in various stages of dress (or undress). In December 2003, A&F placed their winter catalog at each cash register, hoping to up-sell customers on catalog sales after they left the store. Crack the cover and you'll be stunned: kids *without clothes* running free throughout a catalog designed to *sell clothes.* It's soft-core porn. Pictures and articles promoting the glee of group sex. By the way, the target customers for A&F are kids between the ages of twelve and twenty-five. Hmmm.

Recently, Planned Parenthood of Minnesota/South Dakota promoted the "safe sex" mantra by offering "prom survival kits" to high-school graduates before their big night out. The kit included breath mints, confetti, condoms, and a ten-dollar coupon for contraceptive services. According to their education director, Katherine Meerse, "We just wanted to make it a little bit easier for sexually active teens to practice safe sex." How thoughtful![1]

Our culture says sex is safe, normal, and everybody's doing it. They also tell our kids there are no consequences to premarital sex. It's seen on the big screen. It's taught in school. It's reinforced in stores. It's promoted by Planned Parenthood.

> In response, what do most kids hear
> from their parents about sex?
> Not much.

Lie #2: Drugs and Alcohol Are Recreational Novelties

Once again, the entertainment industry is front-and-center in the way it glorifies drug and alcohol use. Our kids see it on television, they watch it at the movies, they hear about it on the radio. Messages from the mainstream media suggest drugs and alcohol are amusing, entertaining, and tranquilizing. These messages normalize drug and alcohol use and minimize their consequences.

Now the facts: according to the Centers for Disease Control and Prevention (CDC), Americans drive under the influence of alcohol about 115 million times a year. The consequences? About 300,000 injuries and 16,000 deaths per year.[2] Unfortunately, about 7,000 of these deaths were innocent moms, dads, and kids whose lives were stolen by drunk drivers. Who's going to convince the surviving family members that there are no consequences to alcohol use?

According to the National Institute on Drug Abuse, 22 percent of eighth graders and nearly half of all twelfth graders have used marijuana. Furthermore, 11 percent of our kids in the eighth grade and 20 percent of our kids in the twelfth grade report using stimulants, inhalants, and hallucinogens in addition to marijuana.[3]

Our culture promotes a mindset to our kids that suggests

drugs and alcohol are harmless recreational activities, and that it's OK to party every once in a while.

> In response, what do most kids hear
> from their parents about drug and alcohol use?
> "Not my kid"

Lie #3: Violence Solves Problems

Survey the movie section of your local newspaper or glance at the TV listing, and tell me what you see. Both confirm the notion that America is being fed a daily diet of violence. As a result many of our kids have become desensitized to violent behavior and fail to recognize its consequences. Within the last twenty years the entertainment industry has sold violence as a recreational activity. Killing has progressed from the big screen to the small screen and now to video games—bringing new meaning to the question, "Got a few hours to kill?"

According to Dr. Craig Anderson, PhD in psychology from Stanford University, research on the effects of violence on kids was renewed with the introduction of electronic video games. Anderson addressed a number of fables with research findings and debunked several common myths:

- *Myth: Research on violent video games has produced mixed results.* Actually, when all relevant empirical studies using meta-analytic techniques are combined, the research identifies three consistent effects of violent games on our kids: increased aggressive behavior, increased physiological arousal, and decreased prosocial (helping) behavior.

- *Myth: No studies directly link violent video games and aggression.* Actually, high levels of violent video exposure have been linked to juvenile delinquency, fighting in school, and violent criminal behavior.

- *Myth: Violent video games affect only a small fraction of kids.* Actually, while it was previously thought that only the most susceptible kids would be influenced by violent video games, the research demonstrated that no subgroup was found to be immune from the negative effects of media violence.

- *Myth: The true effects of violent video games are relatively insignificant.* Actually, a review of the literature reveals that the effects of playing violent video games are actually larger than the effects of secondhand smoke on lung cancer, lead exposure on I.Q. scores in children, and calcium intake on bone mass.[4]

The homicide rate for kids under fifteen in America is five times greater than the rates of twenty-five other industrialized nations combined.[5] Coincidence? Absolutely not. The cultural messages our kids hear from movies, music, television, and video games suggest that violence is a solution, rape is a form of recreation, and consequences are only for those few who get caught.

> In response, what do most kids hear
> from their parents about violence
> in movies, music, and video games?
> Not much.

TRUTH OR CONSEQUENCES

We are in trouble. Our kids are being lied to from the time their feet hit the floor until the time their heads hit the pillow. By parents? No, by a culture that suggests sex is safe, drugs are fun, and violence solves problems. The problem is, when parents fail to stand up and speak out against these lies, our silence is its own kind of lie, reinforcing the lies they've been told.

THE TRUTH

Silence isn't golden. Parents need to be informative, intentional, and initiating when it comes to talking about sex, drugs, and violence. Failing to speak up is as bad as failing to show up.

The first twenty chapters of this book dealt with the lies we've told our kids. They're *lies of commission*—clichés and untruths we've passed on when we've spoken up and shouldn't have. This chapter deals with the three lies we permit the world to tell our kids. By sitting on the sidelines and staying silent, we're committing *lies of omission*. Both kinds of lies will cripple our kids.

Our silence lies to our kids by implying we have no objections to the messages they hear about sex, drugs, and violence. Let me encourage you to step up, stand up, and speak up—starting today. Here are the three messages you need to tell your kids:

1. *There is only one form of "safe sex." It's called abstinence.* Your teachers at school probably won't tell you that.

2. *Drugs and alcohol destroy lives and kill people.* Your friends at school who offer you a drink or a drug probably won't tell you that.

3. *A constant intake of violence desensitizes your mind to the consequences of violence and the value of life.* The research is conclusive: watching violence increases violent behavior. The entertainment industry probably won't tell you that.

> If you don't tell your kids these things,
> You are lying to them by your silence.
> You love them too much to do that.

Jesus put it this way when offering comfort to his companions: "In my Father's house are many room; if it were not so *I would have told you*" (John 14:2). As parents, Jenni and I have followed this model. We tell our kids, "In this world you will hear many lies. If it were not so, we would have told you.

"'Safe sex' is called abstinence—if you need sex to hold a relationship together, it's not much of a relationship.

"Alcohol and drugs are addictive, and they kill people—some faster than others.

"Violence doesn't solve problems—it devalues life and creates greater problems."

> Is it easy to tell our kids these messages?
> No, but it's getting easier.
> How often do we tell our kids these messages?
> Weekly, not weakly.

By the way, remember Michelle, Josh, and Eric? Michelle is now twenty-three years old and has two children. Both were born out of wedlock. Josh received a scholarship to play football at the University of Missouri. He dropped out his junior year due to drug- and alcohol-related problems. And Eric? He never made it past his eighteenth birthday. On April 20, 1999, Eric Harris and Dylan Klebold shot and killed twelve students and one teacher at Columbine High School. Then they committed suicide.

22

THE MOST DAMAGING LIE OF ALL —
The Lie We Tell Ourselves

THIS SHIP IS UNSINKABLE.

Edward J. Smith, captain of the Titanic

After twenty-one chapters of revealing and then wrestling with the lies we tell our kids, it's time for a right turn. It's time for us to confront the lies we tell ourselves. They just may be the most dangerous and damaging of them all.

For some of us a new day means a new delusion. Monday: "I just can't help the way I am." Tuesday: "If I won the lottery, then I'd be happy." Wednesday: "I'm not smart enough to go to college." Thursday: "Next time I'm going to tell them what I really think." Friday: "If only I looked better, then people would like me." Saturday: "Smoking kills people, but it won't kill me." Sunday: "I'm going to start my diet tomorrow."

Next week there will be plenty more lies to choose from:

- "I couldn't do that if I tried."

- "Nobody understands me."

- "I can't control my emotions."

- "I can't stop; I've tried before."

- "Because of my past I'll never be happy."

- "They owe it to me after all I've done for them."

- "One little Oreo cookie won't make a difference."

- "I'm unhappy because of the way people treat me."

- "It's easier to avoid my problems than to face them."

- "If I forgive those people, then I'm condoning their behavior."

- "God doesn't love me. How could he, after what I've done?"

- "Even though I can't afford it, I'll buy it because I deserve it."

- "If only I had their approval, then I would feel good about myself."

The list is long.
The possibilities are endless.
But the worst lie of all is still missing.

The War Within

Three words. That's all it takes. Just like that small smooth stone that David drew from the brook to level a giant named Goliath, this lie will knock you to your knees faster than you can say, "Philistine."

It's a lie that handcuffs you from the minute your feet hit the floor until the moment your head hits the pillow. You see its effects at home and at work, in the family room and in the boardroom. It undermines your marriage and cripples your parenting. It infects the beliefs of the accomplished as well as the apprenticed, the educated as well as the illiterate. More toxic than the bite of a brown recluse spider, this lie ravages the heart of the purposeful and ransacks the spirit of the prayerful.

The lie?
"I don't matter."

Nothing demoralizes us more than the belief that we don't count, that we don't really matter. That we're invisible, pointless, unnecessary.

It's like being the last one picked in gym class—every day. Nobody expects you to make a difference. You're a spare, not a star. While the athletes fight to get in the game, you fight to stay out of the way. The goal is to not be seen, not be heard, not be *there*.

Oh sure, there are times when you think things will be different. But most days you walk through life feeling like you're taking up space—space designed for the fit, the functional, and the fruitful.

It's sad to say, but that's probably how Chris Chubbuck felt.

Chris was a bright, attractive, twenty-nine-year-old talk-show host at WXLT TV in Sarasota, Florida. One Monday morning Chris didn't just report the news; she made it. Just eight minutes into her talk show, "Suncoast Digest," Chris calmly shared with her viewers, "In keeping with Channel Forty's policy of bringing you the latest in blood and guts in living color, we bring you another first—an attempted suicide." With that, she reached into a bag tucked beneath her desk, located a .38 caliber revolver, fired a single shot, and slumped to her desk. She died fourteen hours later in a Sarasota hospital.

In an interview later that day Chris's grief-stricken mother pointed to the likely culprit. She said that Chris had few friends, and even fewer romantic interests.[1]

Insignificant. Irrelevant. Invisible.

Those are the feelings that make the difference between someone living on top of the world . . . and someone living under it. Her peers at the station saw Chris as charming and competent. Chris saw herself as unimportant and unnecessary. Chris believed the lie, and it turned fulfillment into failure.

The lie says you're only as valuable as the clothes you wear, the car you drive, or the balance you carry in your checkbook. The lie says you're significant as a size 2 but disposable as a size 12. The lie says you can protect yourself from hurt and heartache through self-assurance, self-actualization, and self-sufficiency. The lie says that when you're thinner than those around you, richer than those around you, smarter than those around you, younger than those around you, and more accomplished than those around you, *then* you're worth something.

The lie is especially toxic to women. How many? According to research conducted by George Gallop Jr., about 65 percent.[2] That's staggering—but that's how many women struggle with a sense of low self-worth, low self-esteem, and the belief that they don't really matter.

If you could have seen beyond the smile of Judith Bucknell, she could have been the poster child for the IDMS—the "I Don't Matter Society." It was the summer of 1980. Earlier that year socialite Jean Harris shot Doctor Herman Tarnower, creator of the Scarsdale Diet; eight commandos died in a failed attempt to rescue the American Embassy hostages held in Iran; and Mount St. Helens erupted, taking the lives of fifty-seven people. While all were tragic losses of life, Judith Bucknell's death, in some ways, was the most devastating. She died of a broken heart.

June 9 was another hot, humid, hazy day in South Florida. Along with the thermometer, everything was on the rise in Miami: inflation, unemployment, and the crime rate. It was the latter that made the biggest difference to thirty-eight-year-old Judith.

She was murdered on this steamy summer day—stabbed seven times and strangled. To the Miami Police Department she was murder number 106 of the year. As far as I know, her assailant was never caught. A motive was never uncovered. In all likelihood her case found its way to one of the hundreds of unsolved case files that fill the shelves of most metropolitan police departments. But while the case may have gone away, the narrative of Judith's life didn't, thanks to a *Miami Herald* reporter who captured her story and captivated a city.

It turns out that Judith kept a diary, one that described her days, as well as her desires. Unfortunately it painted a picture of a woman with broken dreams and countless disappointments— an epitaph to a lonely life.

Her diary made her seem like one of us. She wrote about getting old, getting fat, and just plain getting by. She wrote about her high points, her low points, and the humdrum days in between. She was successful during the day but floundered after five. She lived a life where much love was offered but little was returned. Her diary had several entries like this one: "Where are the men with the flowers and champagne and music? Where are the men who call and ask for a genuine, actual date? Where are the men who would like to share more than my bed, my booze, my food? . . . I would like to have in my life, once before I pass through my life, the kind of sexual relationship which is part of a loving relationship."

Judith longed to be loved. She longed to have someone with whom she could share her life, not just her bed. A walk in the park? A dinner? A movie? With six billion people on this earth, was that too much to ask?

Sometimes her frustration turned to resentment: "I see people together, and I'm so jealous I want to throw up. What about me? What about me!" Other times it turned to resignation: "I feel so old. Unloved. Unwanted. Abandoned. Used up. I want to cry and sleep forever."

Little did she know, her wish would soon come true.

Months before her murder, Judith began to die. Slowly. One rejection at a time. A one-night stand. A silent telephone. An empty mailbox. Every heartache became a confirmation: "You don't count." Every disappointment became a disgrace: "You don't matter." Every broken dream became a blemish: "You don't fit." From her diary it's obvious: Judith died long before she took her last breath.[3]

Hope for the Hurting

Judith Bucknell died some time ago, but there are millions of others just like her. Maybe you know one. Maybe you saw one this morning—in the mirror.

Like Judith, you don't let on. Few people know. A smile hides your struggle. Your clothes are coordinated, your home is kept, your car is clean—but your life is in shambles. You watch what you eat; you watch what you wear; you watch as life passes you by. Thoughts about your past increase your guilt. Thoughts about your future increase your anxieties. So you keep busy. You run to work; you run to eat; you run to church. Last one in, first one out. No time for small talk. You're too busy . . . hiding.

> Beneath your busyness, you believe the lie:
> You don't matter.

The bad news is: you're not alone. The good news is: you're not alone! Many have preceded you, and many will follow. Some have discovered there is a better way—an antidote to the lie. It's found in focusing on your promise, not your past.

Just ask Aldonza. While paralyzed by her past, she came across a dreamer who offered her a promise. It turns out that he believed in her, even though she didn't believe in herself.

The storyline comes from Dale Wasserman's 1965 musical, *The Man of La Mancha*, which opened on Broadway on November 22, 1965. It ran for 2,328 straight performances. It's a tale of unlimited inspiration, undying dedication, and unbridled optimism. Fast-forward to the scene where the grand idealist, Don Quixote, first meets the prostitute Aldonza. From the moment Quixote sees Aldonza, he thinks she is special. He sees her for what she could be, not what she is.

To Aldonza's amazement, Quixote announces, "You will be my lady." Then he adds, "Yes, you are my lady, and I give you a new name—it's Dulcinea."

The prostitute laughs. She can't see beyond her profession or her pain. A *lady*?

Undaunted, Quixote affirms her and declares his heartfelt belief in her. Aldonza is amused but troubled. She feels like an imposter. A streetwalker in a satin gown. Judas sitting at the table during the Last Supper.

Quixote continues believing in her, despite her resistance.

The next scene: The stage is barren. It's nighttime. From the wing a scream is heard—a scream that would stir the dead. It's Aldonza. She has just been raped. She emerges with her blouse torn and her heart troubled. Her hair is disheveled; her hopes are in disarray. There is dirt on her cheeks and terror in her eyes. Despite her protests during the assault, she is reminded of her past. Her transformation was short-lived.

In a bold but blameless voice, Quixote wraps Aldonza with words of compassion. "My lady," he says. She can't handle the contrast between her plight and his perception. She cries, "Don't call me your lady; I was born in a ditch by a mother who left me there naked and cold and too hungry to cry. I never blamed her . . . I'm sure she left hoping I'd have the sense to die."

Her body is weak. Her spirit is weary. With tears streaming down her cheeks, she screams at Quixote, "Oh, don't call me a lady. I'm only a kitchen hand. Don't call me a lady; I'm only Aldonza. I am nothing at all!" With that she whirls and dashes into the darkness. Quixote responds by shouting into the shadows, "But you are my Lady Dulcinea!"

The curtain drops, and minutes feel like months. (You know what they say about the length of a minute . . . it depends on which side of the bathroom door you're on.) When the curtain rises again, something is wrong. Don Quixote lies dying. Why? Is it a broken body—or a broken heart? Both have been known to steal the breath from the living. He lies there alone, rejected, and ridiculed.

Scorned just like Jesus two thousand years ago.

Suddenly at his side appears a lady. She has the appearance of a Spanish queen; she emanates the splendor of royalty. She kneels and prays for the fallen warrior.

Quixote stirs and whispers, "Who are you?"

"Don't you remember?" she says as she stands. She is beautiful beyond words—proud in her posture yet humble in her presence. Hoping that he would recognize her, she asks again, "Don't you remember? You called me your lady. You gave me a new name. My name is Dulcinea!"[4]

With her declaration, the transformation is complete.

Slowly, gradually, Aldonza had discovered that if the dreamer could believe in the value of the discarded, maybe she could too. A hundred-dollar bill isn't worth any less because it's crumpled. She just needed someone to believe in her.

TRUTH OR CONSEQUENCES

How about you? Are you looking for someone to believe in you?

I know a King who has your name written on his heart. He's an eternal optimist—a divine Don Quixote who believes in you, even when you don't believe in yourself. He loves you as you are and believes in who you can become. He's a dreamer who has a desire for you: " 'For I know the plans I have for you,' declares the LORD, 'plans to prosper you and not to harm you, plans to give you hope and a future' " (Jeremiah 29:11 NIV).

THE TRUTH

Your life matters. You're not insignificant, irrelevant, or inadequate. God believes in you. God values you. And God has a dream for you.

As a matter of fact, God thinks so much of you that he sent his Son to save you, his Spirit to guide you, his Scripture to teach you, and his angels to guard over you. He thinks the world of you. The question is: do you?

Judith Bucknell didn't. She lived the lie. If she had encountered the Almighty, her diary would have read differently because her life would have been lived differently. At some point in her journey with Jesus, she would have stumbled upon his words of promise: "And you shall know the truth, and the truth shall make you free" (John 8:32).

After all, if Jesus can turn water into wine, then he can turn an empty life into an abundant life. He can turn an average parent into an awesome parent. He did both for me . . . and that's no lie.

Notes

Introduction: The Truth about the Lies We Tell

1. James Patterson and Peter Kim, *The Day America Told the Truth: What People Really Believe about Everything That Really Matters* (New York: Plume/Penguin, 1992).

2. U.S. Bureau of Labor Statistics 2000 Census, http://www.census .gov/population/www/index.html; and http://www.bls.gov/home.htm (accessed May 5, 5006).

3. Allison Kornet, "The Truth about Lying: Has Lying Gotten a Bad Rap?" *Psychology Today*, May 1, 1997, 74.

4. Chris Thurman, *The Lies We Believe* (Nashville: Thomas Nelson, 1999), 5–6.

5. Steve Chandler, *Seventeen Lies That Are Holding You Back and the Truth That Will Set You Free* (Los Angeles: Renaissance Books, 2000), 11.

1. Lie: You Can Be Anything You Want to Be

1. Robert Dole, Presidential Nomination Speech, August 15, 1996.

2. Marcus Buckingham and Donald O. Clifton, *Now, Discover Your Strengths* (New York: Free Press, 2001), 7.

3. Arthur Miller Jr., *Why You Can't Be Anything You Want to Be* (Grand Rapids: Zondervan, 1999).

4. "America's 100 Best," ReadersDigest.com, http://www.rd.com/

content/openContent.do?contentId=14809&trkid=rdinsider_may_
05_arch. Follow the link to "Texas" (accessed May 5, 2006).

5. Max Lucado, *Cure for the Common Life: Living in Your Sweet Spot*
(Nashville: W Publishing, 2005), 18.

2. Lie: Looks Don't Matter—It's What's on the Inside That Counts

1. Erich Goode, "Gender and Courtship Entitlement: Responses
to Personal Ads," *Sex Roles: A Journal of Research* 34, no. 3–4 (1996):
144–69.

2. Peter Kilmann and Geoffrey Urbaniak, "Physical Attractiveness
and the 'Nice Guy Paradox': Do Nice Guys Really Finish Last?" *Sex
Roles: A Journal of Research* 49, no. 9–10 (2003): 413.

3. Elaine Hatfield and Susan Sprecher, *Mirror, Mirror: The
Importance of Looks in Everyday Life* (Albany, N.Y.: State University of
New York Press, 1986).

4. Richard Ilkka, "Applicant Appearance and Selection Decision
Making: Revitalizing Employment Interview Education," *Business
Communication Quarterly* 58, no. 3 (1995): 11–28; P. D. Cherulnik,
W. T. Needy, M. Flanagan, and M. Zachau, "Social Skill and Visual
Interaction," *Journal of Social Psychology* 104 (1978): 263–70; and
A. Feingold, "Good Looking People Are Not What We Think,"
Psychological Bulletin 111 (1992): 304–41.

5. C. Crandall and M. Biernat, "The Ideology of Anti-Fat
Attitudes," *Journal of Applied Social Psychology* 20 (1990): 227–43;
and W. DeJong and R. Kleck, "The Social Psychological Effects of
Overweight in Physical Appearance, Stigma and Social Behavior," in
The Ontario Symposium on Personality and Social Psychology, vol. 3, ed.
C. Peter Herman, Mark P. Zanna, and E. Tory Higgins (Hillsdale, N.J.:
Lawrence Erlbaum, 1986), 65–87.

6. V. Ritts, M. Patterson, and M. Tubbs, "Expectations, Impressions,
and Judgments of Physically Attractive Students: A Review," *Review of
Educational Research* 62 (1992): 413–26.

7. K. Hau and F. Salili, "Structure and Semantic Differential
Placement of Specific Causes: Academic Causal Attribution by Chinese
Students in Hong Kong," *International Journal of Psychology* 26 (1992):
175–93.

8. R. Dipboye, R. Arvey, and D. Terpstra, "Sex and Physical
Attractiveness of Raters and Applicants as Determinants of Resume
Evaluation," *Journal of Applied Psychology* 62 (1977): 288–94; R. Dipboye,

H. Fromkin, and K. Wiback, "Relative Importance of Applicant Sex, Attractiveness, and Scholastic Standing in Evaluation of Job Applicant Resume," *Journal of Applied Psychology* 60 (1975): 39–43; and D. Gilmore, T. Beehr, and K. Love, "Effects of Applicant Sex, Applicant Physical Attractiveness, Type of Rater and Type of Job on Interview Decisions," *Journal of Occupational Psychology* 59 (1986): 103–9.

9. N. Hankins, W. McKinnie, and R. Bailey, "Effects of Height, Physique, and Cranial Hair on Job-Related Attributes," *Psychological Reports* 45 (1979): 853–54; and M. Harris, R. Harris, and S. Bochner, "Fat, Four-Eyed, and Female: Stereotypes of Obesity, Glasses, and Gender," *Journal of Applied Social Psychology* 6 (1982): 503–16.

10. Stephanie Armour, "Your appearance, good or bad, can affect size of your paycheck," *USA Today*, July 20, 2005.

11. Bob Minzesheimer, "Blink and you could miss 'the power of thinking without thinking,'" *USA Today*, January 11, 2005, 4D.

12. Charles Stewart and William Cash Jr., *Interviewing: Principles and Practices* (Dubuque, Iowa: William C. Brown, 1994).

13. Mark Knapp and Judith Hall, *Nonverbal Communication in Human Interaction* (Fort Worth: Holt, Rinehart and Winston, 1992), 9.

3. Lie: Life Is Fair

1. Mark Buchanan, "Life Is Unfair (and That's OK)," *Christianity Today*, April 23, 2001, 92.

2. Aliea's story can be found on the Mothers Against Drunk Driving Web site, http://www.madd.org/victims/6415 (accessed May 5, 2006).

3. Bob Herbert, "Justice takes its time for innocent man," *New York Times*, January 6, 2004.

4. Doug Herman, *FaithQuake: Rebuilding Your Faith after Tragedy Strikes* (Grand Rapids: Baker, 2003).

5. *USA Today*, "Maid pardoned for killing—60 years late," August 31, 2005.

6. Lauren Terrazzano, "Yale student's homeless years taught him to adapt," (Ft. Worth) *Star-Telegram*, July 11, 2004, 10A.

4. Lie: It's the Thought That Counts

1. Gary Chapman, *The Five Love Languages: How to Express Heartfelt Commitment to Your Mate* (Chicago: Moody), 1993.

5. Lie: It Doesn't Matter Whether You Win or Lose—It's How You Play the Game

1. Vince Lombardi, speech from the Official Site of Vince Lombardi, copyright the Estate of Vince Lombardi, c/o CMG Worldwide, www .vincelombardi.com/about/speech.html (accessed May 5, 2006).

2. Chris Bury, host, "A Winning Obsession," *Nightline*, ABC News, August 20, 2004.

3. Associated Press, "Will lawyers be the next olympians?" October 1, 2000, http://espn.go.com/oly/summer00/news/2000/1001/795892 .html (accessed May 5, 2006).

4. Bury, "A Winning Obsession."

6. Lie: God Helps Those Who Help Themselves

1. CTV.ca News Staff, "Climber recounts tale of amputating his own arm," May 8, 2003, http://www.ctv.ca/servlet/ArticleNews/story/ CTVNews/20030508/aronralston_climberamputee_20030508/20030508/ (accessed May 5, 2006).

2. Mark Jenkins, "Aron Ralston—Between a Rock and the Hardest Place," *Outside Online*, August 23, 2003, http://outside.away.com/ outside/features/200308/200308_hardway_200308_1.html (accessed May 5, 2006).

3. CNN.com, "Nursing home owners face charges," September 13, 2005, http://www.cnn.com/2005/US/09/13/katrina.impact/ (accessed May 5, 2006).

4. Laura Parker, "What really happened at St. Rita's?" *USA Today*, November 28, 2005, http://www.usatoday.com/news/nation/2005-11 -28-st-ritas_x.htm?POE=NEWISVA.

5. "Born Again Christians Ignorant of Faith: Survey Also Finds Hell's Description Divides Americans," Barna Research Outline, March 18, 1995, 1.

6. Aesop's Fables, http://www.pubwire.com/downloaddocs/Afables .PDF (accessed May 5, 2006).

7. Erwin W. Lutzer, *Ten Lies about God and How You Might Already Be Deceived* (Nashville: Word, 2000), 175.

8. Ibid.

9. Ibid.

7. Lie: Love Will Last a Lifetime

1. The Wedding Report, "U.S. Wedding Market Overview," http://

www.theweddingreport.com/ (accessed May 5, 2006).

2. Zeke Quezada, "The Las Vegas Wedding: Getting Married Without a Hitch," http://govegas.about.com/od/lasvegaswedding/a/lvwedding.html (accessed May 5, 2006).

3. Americans for Divorce Reform, "Divorce Rates," http://www.divorcereform.org/rates.html#anchor168283 (accessed May 5, 2006).

4. U.S. Census Bureau, Population Division, Marriage and Family Statistics Branch, "Marriage, Divorce and Remarriage in the 1990's," Current Population Reports, (Washington, DC: U.S. Government Printing Office, 1992), 23–180.

5. "Love Will Keep Us Together," http://www.songfacts.com/detail.php?id=1810 (accessed May 5, 2006).

6. Matthew D. Bramlett and William D. Mosher, "Cohabitation, Marriage, Divorce and Remarriage in the United States" (National Center for Health Statistics, Vital and Health Statistics 23, no. 22, 2002); and Americans for Divorce Reform, http://www.divorcereform.org/real.html (accessed May 5, 2006).

7. J. Hattie, J. Myers, J. Rosen-Grandon, "The Relationship between Marital Characteristics, Marital Interaction Processes, and Marital Satisfaction," *Journal of Counseling and Development* 82 (2004).

8. Uexpress.com, Dear Abby, "Friendship Is on the Rocks over Case of Wedding Wine," http://www.uexpress.com/dearabby/?uc_full_date=20010224 (accessed May 5, 2006).

9. Michael J. McManus, *Marriage Savers: Helping Your Friends and Family Avoid Divorce* (Grand Rapids: Zondervan, 1995), 22.

8. Lie: Leaders Are Born, Not Bred

1. "Presidential Prerequisites," *INFOsearch: Current Thoughts and Trends Encyclopedia.* Compact disc, version 4.2. The Computer Assistant, 1998.

2. "Mother Teresa of Calcutta: Peacemaker, Pioneer, Legend," EWTN Global Catholic Network, http://www.ewtn.com/motherteresa/ (accessed May 5, 2006).

3. "Battle of Amiens and General A. W. Currie: A Greater Triumph," Canada's Digital Collections, http://collections.ic.gc.ca/heirloom_series/volume4/160-161.html; and "Lieutenant-General Sir Arthur Currie," http://www.worldwar1.com/bioccurr.htm (accessed May 5, 2006).

4. Ralph M. Stogdill, "Personal Factors Associated with Leadership: A Survey of the Literature," *Journal of Psychology* 25 (1948): 35–71.

5. John C. Maxwell, *The Twenty-One Irrefutable Laws of Leadership: Follow Them and People Will Follow You* (Nashville: Thomas Nelson, 1998), 23.

6. "Attractive Lights," *INFOsearch: Illustrations Encyclopedia.* Compact disc, version 4.2. The Computer Assistant, 1998.

7. "Lead from Among," *INFOsearch: Illustrations Encyclopedia.*

8. "A Cause," *INFOsearch: Illustrations Encyclopedia.*

9. "This Is a Football!" *INFOsearch: Illustrations Encyclopedia.*

10. "Wagonmaster or Engineer?" *INFOsearch: Illustrations Encyclopedia.*

11. "Pulling Power," *INFOsearch: Illustrations Encyclopedia.*

12. "Making a Difference," *INFOsearch: Illustrations Encyclopedia.*

9. Lie: Your Past Determines Your Future

1. Tony Lee, "2002: Rating the Nation's Best and Worst Jobs," CareerJournal.com, http://www.careerjournal.com/jobhunting/change/20020507-lee.html (accessed May 5, 2006).

2. Occupational Outlook Handbook, U.S. Department of Labor, Bureau of Labor Statistics, Actuaries, February 27, 2004, http://www.bls.gov/oco/ocos041.htm (accessed May 5, 2006).

3. Cheryl Green, *Child of Promise: One Woman's Journey from Tragedy to Triumph* (Nashville: Broadman & Holman, 2001).

4. Reynaldo Geronimo, "Taking a Leaf from Nida's Last Will and Testament," The Trust Guru, http://www.thetrustguru.com/today112601.htm (accessed May 5, 2006).

5. Kenneth L. Woodward, "What Miracles Mean," *Newsweek*, May 1, 2000.

10. Lie: You Can Have It All

1. "Yuppies: The Social Class that Loves to Buy," *Newsweek*, December 31, 1984, 14–24.

2. "The *Our Gang* Curse? The Painful Lives of the *Our Gang* Cast Members—Truth! and Fiction!" TruthOrFiction.com, http://www.truthorfiction.com/rumors/o/ourgang.htm (accessed May 5, 2006).

3. Lindsay Young, "The Big Bankruptcy Squeeze," BizNewOrleans.com, June 15, 2005, http://bizneworleans.com/70+M50f5273b6dc.html (accessed May 5, 2006).

4. Adapted from "Five More Minutes—Please?" Epinions.com, http://www.epinions.com/content_2197659780 (September 26, 2001. Updated October 31, 2001) (accessed May 5, 2006).

11. Lie: It's Not What You Know but Who You Know That Counts

1. "Tori Spelling," Internet Movie Database Inc., http://www.imdb
.com/name/nm0001760/ (accessed May 5, 2006).

2. Robert Kuttner, "The Voice of Privilege," *Boston Globe*, January 22, 2003, A15.

3. "Success related to work," Bible.org, http://www.bible.org/illus
.asp?topic_id=1065 (accessed May 5, 2006).

4. Laura Koss-Feder, "In job search, it's often who you know," *New York Times*, February 10, 1997, 13.

5. Elizabeth Winter, "CPA—The 90,000 Rule," *Canadian Corporate News*, Toronto, November 20, 2003.

12. Lie: Don't Talk to Strangers—or You'll Be Sorry

1. The Federal Bureau of Investigation, U.S. Department of Justice, http://www.fbi.gov/mostwant/kidnap/lebron.htm (accessed May 5, 2006).

2. The Federal Bureau of Investigation, U.S. Department of Justice, http://www.fbi.gov/mostwant/kidnap/patterson.htm (accessed May 5, 2006).

3. The Federal Bureau of Investigation, U.S. Department of Justice, http://www.fbi.gov/mostwant/kidnap/kraft.htm (accessed May 5, 2006).

4. Kathleen W. Zoehfeld, *Don't Talk to Strangers, Pooh!* (New York: Scholastic, 1998).

5. Robert Fulghum, *All I Really Need to Know I Learned in Kindergarten* (New York: Random House, 1988).

6. National Center for Missing and Exploited Children, 2005, "Frequently Asked Questions and Statistics," http://www
.ncmec.org/missingkids/servlet/PageServlet?LanguageCountry=en_
US&PageId=242 (accessed May 5, 2006).

7. David Finkelhor, Heather Hammer, and Andrea J. Sedlak, "Nonfamily Abducted Children: National Estimates and Characteristics," *NISMART*, U.S. Department of Justice, Office of Juvenile Justice and Delinquency Prevention, October 2002, http://www.ncmec.org/en_US/
documents/nismart2_nonfamily.pdf (accessed May 5, 2006).

8. Gavin De Becker, *Protecting the Gift: Keeping Children and Teenagers Safe (And Parents Sane)* (New York: Dial, 1999).

9. Tom Kenworthy, "With boy safe, searchers celebrate," *USA Today*, June 22, 2005.

10. Kenworthy, "Lost Utah boy hid from rescuers, fearing strangers," *USA Today*, June 23, 2005.

13. Lie: If You Have Talent, You're Bound to Go Far in Life

1. Associated Press, "Child prodigy, 14, kills self," *The Washington Times*, March 20, 2005, http://www.washtimes.com/national/20050319 -114815-3232r.htm (accessed May 5, 2006).

2. Brad Cesmat, "The Story of Todd Marinovich,"AZFamily.com, http://www.azfamily.com/sports/brad_cesmat/stories/KTVKBrad20050527 .2b6c9fb13.html (accessed May 5, 2006).

3. "Bobby Fisher," Wikipedia, The Free Encyclopedia, http:// wikipedia.org/wiki/Bobby_Fisher#Playing_career_before_1967 (accessed May 5, 2006).

4. Yang Li and Ken Gerold, "High and Low IQ," Thinkquest, http:// library.thinkquest.org/C0121653/extrema.htm (accessed May 5, 2006).

5. "David Farragut," Wikipedia, http://en.wikipedia.org/wiki/ David_Farragut (accessed May 5, 2006).

6. "Murray Gell-Mann," Wikipedia, http://en.wikipedia.org/wiki/ Murray_Gell-Mann (accessed May 5, 2006).

7. "Nadia Comaneci," Wikipedia, http://en.wikipedia.org/wiki/ Nadia_Comaneci (accessed May 5, 2006).

8. "Stevie Wonder," Wikipedia, http://en.wikipedia.org/wiki/ Stevie_Wonder (accessed May 5, 2006).

9. "Dakota Fanning," NetGlimse, http://www.netglimse.com/ celebs/pages/dakota_fanning/index.shtml (accessed May 5, 2006).

10. *TIME Asia*, "Famous Flameouts," http://www.time.com/time/ asia/covers/501030217/flameouts.html (accessed May 5, 2006).

11. "Famous Flameouts."

12. "Famous Flameouts."

13. Chuck and Jenni Borsellino, *How to Raise Totally Awesome Kids* (Sisters, Ore.: Multnomah, 2002), 56–60.

14. Lie: It Doesn't Matter What You Do in Life, as Long as You're
Happy

1. Karen Goldberg Goff, "Start early, leave later." *Washington Times*, Sept. 28, 2003, http://www.washtimes.com/familytimes/20030927 -112318-5070r.htm (accessed May 5, 2006).

2. CNN.com, "Atlanta hostage: 'I wanted to gain his trust,'" March 14, 2005, http://www.cnn.com/2005/LAW/03/13/cnna.smith/;

"Nichols to make court appearance today," March 15, 2005, www.cnn
.com/2005/LAW/03/14/atlanta.shooting/; and "Reward up to $40,000
for woman who turned in Nichols," March 16, 2005, www.cnn.
com/2005/LAW/03/16/atlanta.shooting/ (accessed May 5, 2006).

3. You can find these Bible stories in Genesis 28 (Jacob), 1 Kings 3
(Solomon), and Genesis 37 (Joseph).

4. See Psalm 139:16, 14; and Jeremiah 29:11.

15. Lie: It's Not Your Fault

1. Consumer Attorneys of California, "Real Facts in McDonalds
Hot Coffee Case," (Fresno, Calif., 1995–1996), FreeRepublic.com,
www.FreeRepublic.com/forum/a3b77256026e6.htm (accessed May 5,
2006).

2. Center for Consumer Freedom, "Special Report: 'The first thing
we do, let's kill all the lawyers,'" (Washington, D.C., July 26, 2002),
http://www.consumerfreedom.com/news_detail.cfm/headline/1500
(accessed May 5, 2006).

3. Ask Yahoo, "What is the 'Twinkie Defense'?"(August 29, 2001),
http://ask.yahoo.com/20010829.html (accessed May 5, 2006).

16. Lie: Of Course There's a Santa Claus

1. About.com, "Priest informs kids that Santa doesn't exist,"
Pasadena Star-News, http://atheism.about.com/b/a/127802.htm
(accessed May 5, 2006).

2. These letters are based on correspondence or stories I have
collected over the years from patients, newspaper articles, and the
Internet.

3. Carleton Kendrick, "Family Therapy Question and Answer," The
Family Education Network, http://www.familyeducation.com/experts/
advice/0,1183,1-4289,00.html (accessed May 5, 2006).

4. Holy Trinity Lutheran Church, (Hacienda Heights, Calif.),
"The Gospel According to Santa Clause," September 13, 2003, http://
holytrinity.ms/the_gospel_according_to_santa_clause.htm (accessed
May 5, 2006).

5. Gary Grassl, "Does Santa Harm Children?" 2think.org, http://
www.2think.org/hii/santa.shtml (accessed May 5, 2006).

17. Lie: Busy Kids Are Happy Kids

1. Cheryl Wetzstein, "Students active even after class; Study:

Parents give vital push," *Washington Times*, November 16, 2004, http://www.findarticles.com/p/articles/mi_go1637/is_200411/ai_n7467673.

2. Joan Whitely, "In Depth: Stress Check," *Las Vegas Review-Journal*, March 4, 2001, http://www.reviewjournal.com/lvrj_home/2001/Mar-04-Sun-2001/news/15071476.html (accessed May 5, 2006).

3. Alvin Rosenfeld and Nicole Wise, *The Over-Scheduled Child: Avoiding the Hyper-Parenting Trap* (New York: St. Martin's Griffin, 2000).

4. Whitely, "In Depth: Stress Check."

5. Rosenfeld and Wise, *The Over-Scheduled Child*.

6. David Elkind, *The Hurried Child: Growing Up Too Fast Too Soon* (Cambridge, Mass.: Perseus, 2001).

7. Alvin Rosenfeld, interview by Matt Lauer, April 21, 2005, "Raising Kids Today," *The Today Show*, http://www.hyper-parenting.com/today.htm (accessed May 5, 2006).

8. Jane Christmas, "The Kids Are Not Alright," Balancetv.ca, http://www.balancetv.ca/balancetv/client/en/Simplify_Special/DetailNews.asp?idNews=370&pg=2&pgL= (accessed May 5, 2006).

9. Christmas, "The Kids Are Not Alright," Balancetv.ca, http://www.balancetv.ca/balancetv/client/en/Simplify_Special/DetailNewsPrint.asp?id=370 (accessed May 5, 2006).

10. "What Do You Do For Fun?" *Business Week*, May 24, 2004, http://www.businessweek.com/magazine/content/04_21/b3884138_mz070.htm (accessed May 5, 2006).

11. Karen Goldberg Goff, "Start early, leave later," *Washington Times*, September 28, 2003, http://www.washtimes.com/familytimes/20030927-112318-5070r.htm (accessed May 5, 2006).

12. Goldberg Goff, "Start early, leave later."

13. David Elkind, "Are We Pushing Our Kids Too Hard?" *Psychology Today*, January 1, 2003, http://www.psychologytoday.com/articles/pto-2613.html (accessed May 5, 2006).

14. Nicholas Zill, Christine Winquist Nord, and Laura Spencer Loomis, "Adolescent Time Use, Risky Behavior and Outcomes: An Analysis of National Data," http://aspe.hhs.gov/hsp/cyp/xstimuse.htm (accessed May 5, 2006).

15. Whitely, "In Depth: Stress Check."

16. Elkind, "Are We Pushing Our Kids Too Hard?"

17. Sarah Sabaratnam, "The overscheduled child," *New Straits Times*, September 6, 2000, Life and Times Sec., 2.

18. Elkind, "Are We Pushing Our Kids Too Hard?"

19. Cathy Booth Thomas, "The Push to Be Perfect," *Time*, August 8, 2005, 59.

18. Lie: All *Good Things Come in Small Packages*

1. "World's smallest baby born in US," BBC News, December 21, 2004, http://news.bbc.co.uk/1/hi/world/americas/4116665.stm (accessed May 5, 2006).

2. Allan Dell, "Sara Webster proves she can hang in there with the big boys," (Sarasota, Fla.) *Herald Tribune*, January 23, 2003.

3. Dell, "Sara Webster."

4. Adapted from Bruce Wilkinson, *The Dream Giver* (Sisters, Ore.: Multnomah, 2003). I can't say enough about this book. Read it and you'll be rejuvenated to live out God's dream for your life.

5. Lakewood Public Library, Women in History, Wilma Rudolph biography, http://www.lkwdpl.org/wihohio/rudo-wil.htm (accessed August 12, 2005); and Mary Beth Roberts, "Rudolph ran and world went wild," ESPN, http://espn.go.com/classic/biography/s/Rudolph_Wilma.html (accessed May 5, 2006).

19. Lie: *The Best Things in Life Are Free*

1. Adapted from Jim Stovall, "The Mountain," Afterhours Inspirational Stories, http://www.inspirationalstories.com/0/31.html (accessed May 5, 2006).

20. Lie: *If It Doesn't Kill You, It Will Make You Stronger*

1. Kathy Troccoli, *Am I Still Not God?* (Nashville: W Publishing, 2002).

2. Robert Wicks, "Friedrich Nietzsche," *The Stanford Encyclopedia of Philosophy*, http://plato.stanford.edu/archives/fall2004/entries/nietzsche/ (accessed May 5, 2006).

3. Victor and Mildred Goertzel, "Cradles of Eminence," *INFOsearch: Current Thoughts and Trends Encyclopedia*. Compact disc, version 4.2. The Computer Assistant, 1998.

4. Robert Schuller, *Tough Times Never Last, but Tough People Do!* (New York: Random House/Bantam Books, 1984).

5. James Brady, "In Step with Olivia Newton-John," *Parade*, Sept 11, 2005.

6. Troccoli, *Am I Still Not God?* 174.

7. Steve Young, *Great Failures of the Extremely Successful: Mistakes, Adversity, Failure and Other Steppingstones to Success* (Los Angeles: Tallfellow, 2002).

8. Rebecca Renner, "Nietzsche's Toxicology—whatever doesn't kill you might make you stronger," *Scientific American*, August 18, 2003, http://www.sciam.com/article.cfm?articleID=00019A70-0C1C-1F41 -B0B980A841890000 (accessed May 5, 2006).

9. Renner, "Nietzsche's Toxicology."

10. Renner, "Nietzsche's Toxicology."

11. See Matthew 9:20–22.

12. Troccoli, *Am I Still Not God?*

21. Lie: Silence Is Golden

1. Elisa Klein, "In Focus: Be Prepared for Prom!" Teenwire.com, May 4, 2004, http://www.teenwire.com/infocus/2004/if-20040504p286 -prom.php (accessed May 5, 2006).

2. Richard Carmona, U.S. surgeon general, U.S. Department of Health and Human Services (speech, Public Safety Wellness Week, Orlando, Florida, January 22, 2003), http://www.surgeongeneral.gov/ news/speeches/publicsafewell.htm (accessed May 5, 2006).

3. Patrick Zickler, "Drug use among America's teenagers shows slight downward trend," National Institute on Drug Abuse, *NIDA Notes* 14, no.1 (April, 1999), http://www.drugabuse.gov/NIDA_Notes/ NNVol14N1/teenagers.html (accessed May 5, 2006).

4. Craig Anderson, "Violent Video Games: Myths, Facts, and Unanswered Questions," *Psychological Science Agenda* 16, no 5 (October, 2005), APA Online, http://www.apa.org/science/psa/sb-andersonprt .html (accessed May 5, 2006).

5. Carmona, speech.

22. Lie: The Most Damaging Lie of All

1. Christine Chubbuck." Wikipedia, The Free Encyclopedia, http:// en.wikipedia.org/wiki/Chris_Chubbuck (accessed May 5, 2006).

2. Nancy Stafford, *Beauty by the Book: Seeing Yourself as God Sees You* (Sisters, Ore.: Multnomah, 2002).

3. This story was described in the book *No Wonder They Call Him the Savior: Chronicles of the Cross* by Max Lucado (Sisters, Ore.: Multnomah, 1986). Since then it has appeared in several sources. If

you haven't read the works of Max Lucado, you're missing a treat. He's a surgeon with words and one of the best storytellers since the Greatest Storyteller of all—Jesus.

4. Adapted from Dale Wasserman, *Man of La Mancha: A Musical Play* (New York: Dell, 1965).